T0236328

Getting the Most out of
Node.js Frameworks

Getting the Most out of Node.js Frameworks

The Essential Tools and Libraries

Sufyan bin Uzayr

CRC Press
Taylor & Francis Group
Boca Raton London New York

CRC Press is an imprint of the
Taylor & Francis Group, an **informa** business

First edition published 2022
by CRC Press
6000 Broken Sound Parkway NW, Suite 300, Boca Raton, FL 33487-2742

and by CRC Press
2 Park Square, Milton Park, Abingdon, Oxon, OX14 4RN

CRC Press is an imprint of Taylor & Francis Group, LLC

© 2022 Sufyan bin Uzayr

ISBN: 9781032067568 (hbk)
ISBN: 9781032067537 (pbk)
ISBN: 9781003203711 (ebk)

DOI: 10.1201/9781003203711

Typeset in Minion Pro
by KnowledgeWorks Global Ltd.

For Dad

Contents

Acknowledgments

There are many people who deserve to be on this page, for this book would not have come into existence without their support. That said, some names deserve a special mention, and I am genuinely grateful to:

- My parents, for everything they have done for me.

- My siblings, for helping with things back home.

- The Parakozm team, especially Aruzhan Nuraly and Madina Karybzhanova, for offering great amounts of help and assistance during the book-writing process.

- The CRC team, especially Sean Connelly and Jessica Vega, for ensuring that this book's content, layout, formatting and everything else remains perfect throughout.

- Reviewers of this book, for going through the manuscript and providing their insight and feedback.

- Typesetters, cover designers, printers, and everyone else, for their part in the development of this book.

- All the folks associated with Zeba Academy, either directly or indirectly, for their help and support.

- The programming community in general, and the web development community in particular, for all their hard work and efforts.

Sufyan bin Uzayr

About the Author

Sufyan bin Uzayr is a writer, coder and entrepreneur with more than a decade of experience in the industry. He has authored several books in the past, pertaining to a diverse range of topics, ranging from History to Computers/IT.

Sufyan is the Director of Parakozm, a multinational IT company specializing in EdTech solutions. He also runs Zeba Academy, an online learning and teaching vertical with a focus on STEM fields.

Sufyan specializes in a wide variety of technologies, such as JavaScript, Dart, WordPress, Drupal, Linux and Python. He holds multiple degrees, including ones in Management, IT, Literature and Political Science.

Sufyan is a digital nomad, dividing his time between four countries. He has lived and taught in universities and educational institutions around the globe. Sufyan takes a keen interest in technology, politics, literature, history and sports, and in his spare time, he enjoys teaching coding and English to young students.

Learn more at sufyanism.com.

CHAPTER 1

Introduction to JavaScript Frameworks

If you've had any experience with JavaScript (JS), you must have already come across the term "JavaScript frameworks." What exactly are these JS frameworks that everyone keeps talking about? And what speciality do they bring to development?

While nowadays there is a tendency to label almost every other project as a "framework," there are certain key characteristics that are required in order for a piece of code to be termed a "framework." In the world of JS, there is no dearth of frameworks and libraries.

As you progress through the chapters of this book, you will be introduced to some of the most popular, innovative, and specialized JS frameworks. You will learn details pertaining to installation and setup as well as best practices and methods to get the most out of these JS frameworks.

With that said, before going further, it is a good idea to learn a bit about frameworks in general. As mentioned above, sometimes many concepts or libraries are incorrectly termed as JS frameworks.

To avoid making such mistakes, let us spend a moment familiarizing ourselves with what JS frameworks are, what they can do (and what they cannot), and how you should consider using them.

In this chapter, we will not only be covering what is meant by JS frameworks, but also look at how such frameworks are distinguished from libraries, what are their major uses, and when should or shouldn't you be using one.

DOI: 10.1201/9781003203711-1   1

WHAT ARE JS FRAMEWORKS?

First, let us start our discussion by figuring out what exactly are JS frameworks.

In the simplest of words, a JS framework is an application-level entity that is used to define or put together the entire application design.

Confusing? Put it this way: A JS framework is a collection of components and code blocks that are required to perform a specific set of functions and actions. In other words, a JS framework is a body of predefined code that you can apply or use in your projects by combining it with your own code.

In this manner, a JS framework eliminates burden from the developer's side by calling its various methods and components to perform particular functions. Note that here the developer's code does not call the framework—it is the other way round. The JS framework outlines the guiding concepts for a given type of application (say, a single page web app) and the actual code can be modeled around the same.

Naturally, depending on the level, complexity and amount of functions that a given JS framework can handle, it can be a really big one or a rather small framework meant for a very specific niche task. Smaller or less-generic JS frameworks are often dubbed as libraries—a key difference that we will turn to later in this chapter.

Now, to better understand how a JS framework functions, consider this: Say, you can see that we have our own code that is meant to perform a given role. However, it cannot function in its present state as it requires further functions, dependencies, libraries, etc. We have two options: We can code it all by ourselves and save hours and days working on it, or we can make use of a readymade JS framework that contains a predefined set of code which will perform the dependent actions required for our code to function. By combining the JS framework with the prewritten code, we can easily get the job done and save a good deal of coding time.

HOW ARE JS FRAMEWORKS DIFFERENT FROM LIBRARIES?

Now that we have discussed what JS frameworks are, it is time to turn our attention to another entity that is often (incorrectly) used interchangeably with frameworks—JS libraries.

A library is a set of tools and code methods that help you perform particular tasks. On the other hand, a framework is more of a guideline that directs how you should present your code. The framework is generally not called by your code—instead, it is the JS framework that calls the code. Whatever application you build, the code is structurally defined by the JS framework at large.

More often than not, many programmers find the distinction between libraries and frameworks to be rather blurry. However, it is not really that difficult. A JS framework will tell you how your project or application is to be structured. A JS library is just a set of components and blocks that you can use to perform a series of tasks within the said project or application.

JS libraries tend to be fairly easier to incorporate in projects. Irrespective of your coding methodology, you can work with JS libraries such as jQuery and incorporate them in your project with ease. JS frameworks, however, are often demanding in terms of implementation and organization.

It is generally a better idea to use a JS framework right from the start of a project and model your project around the framework, say Angular. While you can easily incorporate a new library in an existing project, implementing a new framework in an existing project is often tricky business and requires quite a good deal of effort.

Thus, we can safely claim that JS libraries are more flexible than JS frameworks.

Now, to better understand how each can be used by your projects, consider this simple illustration: Let us assume that we are planning to build a JS application that acts as a calculator and performs basic mathematical functions. However, for each result, say addition or subtraction, it shows an animation when displaying the output.

As you can see, your code makes use of the JS library and calls its various functions or methods for a series of tasks, in this case, animations. The library itself is contained with the JS framework, which in turn calls your code to build the application, in this case, the calculator. This is a very simplified and straightforward example to help you comprehend how and where do JS frameworks fit in the bigger picture.

To simplify things, we can state that JS libraries are pretty much collections of classes and methods. The best and most obvious purpose of such libraries is the ability to reuse existing code and save time and efforts therein. A framework, on the other hand, provides a skeleton using which your app can define its own features that will be called by the framework as and when required.

Of late, certain JS libraries such as Prototype have evolved to such common level usage that they are clubbed under frameworks and libraries both. We will turn to this concept later on in this book when we discuss Prototype. For now, it will do well to remember the following:

- A library is called by the code, whereas the JS framework itself calls the code.

- A JS framework is a semi-complete entity that provides a skeletal structure for your code to be based around it, to suit a given purpose or need. A library, unlike a framework, is a collection of functions that can be used by your project to perform just a particular set of tasks.

PROS AND CONS OF JS FRAMEWORKS

Understanding or assessing the pros and cons of JS frameworks is fairly easy, especially if you have any level of background in development.

The good part associated with any JS framework is that you get a solid foundation to begin with. Most decent JS frameworks tend to come with a robust and very reliable code base that is always under active development. Bug fixes, security updates and everything else is readily available.

This, naturally, takes a good deal of headache out of development. You do not have to worry about writing anything from the ground up—you already have a solid foundation that the JS framework provides and you can build your project on top of it.

Beyond that, there are various ostensible benefits associated with JS frameworks too. First, most of the major JS frameworks tend to have a very loyal and active community. This means if you ever run into a bug or trouble with your project, help is always at hand from fellow users of the same JS framework.

Second, new updates and patches are applied fairly faster to JS frameworks—especially if the community is active. This means your project rests on good shoulders.

Third, it is generally time-saving and easier to code with the help of a JS framework than it is to do so without one. It can save coding hours and efforts by providing you with a preexisting code base to work with.

So to sum it up, JS frameworks bring the following advantages to the table:

- **Efficient Coding:** This is made possible due to the existence of a robust code base and solid coding standards that every decent JS framework tends to provide.

- **Saves Time/Money/Efforts:** Simply by providing you with a solid foundation to build your project on, the framework can save a great deal of time in the long run.

- **Better Security/Updates:** The community never sleeps! JS frameworks such as React, Angular, or VueJS have a very loyal user that is always happy to report problems and issues, help out new users and assist you with any queries that you may have!

- **Terrific Documentation:** Even if the official docs are lacking, many of the major JS frameworks have a very effective literature available on the internet that can make learning fun again.

But does this mean JS frameworks have no shortcomings? Of course not. Depending on your requirements and preferences, you might at times find JS frameworks to be lacking in certain aspects.

To begin with, any JS framework, no matter how lightweight and nimble it is, is generally slower to run as compared to raw JS. This means you are compromising, in some way or the other, in terms of speed.

But the biggest flaw, arguably, associated with JS frameworks is that migration is not always the easiest thing to do. When you pick a JS framework for your project, migrating to a different framework down the road will surely be a challenging task, if not outright difficult. While for the most part you are safe and do not need to migrate away from a JS framework, what if the said framework goes out of development?

This generally happens with smaller and lesser-known frameworks (and not React or Angular). If the community or developers lose interest, bug fixes and security patches may be hard to come by. This means your project will rest on obsolete code—naturally, migration to another framework will only be the logical choice.

In this manner, opting for a JS framework can sometimes be limiting for many developers. This is why many "expert" coders tend to go with a framework-less approach. But of course, this is just one side of the story. At times, you need to save your coding time. Other times, using a JS framework simply means you are not trying to reinvent the wheel but instead opting for a standardized coding standard that will ensure your application complies with the best coding practices. Just because a given software, say Mac OS, may go out of development decades from now does not mean you cannot use it today. Technology is an ever-evolving concept and so are JS frameworks.

With that said, if your workflow feels better sans a framework, perhaps you should use JS frameworks only sparingly or occasionally, and focus more on vanilla JS.

Wait, vanilla JS? What's that? Let us now turn our attention to a framework vs framework-less world comparison.

JS FRAMEWORKS VS VANILLA JS

What is vanilla JS? In simple words, it refers to plain, raw JS without an active framework. For the sake of clarity, one can even just refer to it as "pure" JS, albeit that term is often viewed as a misnomer—frameworks in JS are not an impurity.

However, what benefit does working without a JS framework really have? There are a lot of arguments that can be made both for and against using JS without frameworks. For instance, it can be argued that raw JS gives you better control and helps you command your project's direction and glow exactly the way you want.

For advanced and experienced coders, this might indeed be true. Sometimes, control over the app is really desirable, especially if the framework you are working with is highly opinionated (such as Angular). Using raw JS means you are not bound by the standards of a given framework and have better room for experimentation.

On the downside, using JS sans frameworks surely has a steeper and comparatively more difficult learning curve. You do not have access to the framework's community literature or documentation. Plus, following the framework-approach for development is often easier for absolute beginners as they have a preexisting foundation to work with. In plain JS, no such luxury exists.

But the above points are rather minor arguments. In favor of JS frameworks, it can be said that the best use is when you are working with user interface (UIs). Using raw JS for UI development is often complicated and at times even confusing—as we progress through the chapters of this book and you are introduced to JS frameworks especially meant for such tasks, you will notice just how difficult life can be without such frameworks.

And the biggest argument against JS frameworks? If you have working knowledge of plain JS, you can consider yourself framework-proof even if you rely on a given set of frameworks. Consider this: Nowadays, a good number of jQuery developers are learning and trying to catch up with React or Angular. Why is this so? Because the latter options have risen in popularity.

However, for pure JS developers that does not rely always on one framework. Such catching up is easier to accomplish. You can build an app in VueJS or Meteor without gaining mastery over these frameworks, only if you have a sound knowledge of JS in itself.

As such, even if you work with JS frameworks, it is often advisable to keep your JS abilities in good shape and spend some time going back and learning plain JS. This will, effectively, ensure that you are not limited to a particular standard within a particular framework but have greater room for flexibility and growth.

But How Do You Do This?

It's fairly simple, actually. As you code through your projects in any JS framework of your choosing, you should also consider asking yourself what would the equivalent code be, perchance you were not using a JS framework? More importantly, how would you be doing it if the said JS framework were replaced by another one?

In some of the chapters of this book, we will be discussing code samples comparatively so as to better comprehend the difference and also to get a firmer grasp over plain JS. At this stage, it might seem daunting to you especially if you are a beginner to the world of JS. But once you have understood the basics, it will be very easy to pass from one stage to another.

Now that we have talked a good deal about JS frameworks, we can safely turn our attention to one final query.

WHY AND WHEN SHOULD YOU USE A JS FRAMEWORK?

At this point, we have covered what frameworks are, how they differ from libraries in JS, and what benefits or drawbacks they provide.

Now, on to the bigger questions: Why should you use a JS framework? And when to pick which one?

The "why" part must be easier to answer. We have already covered the many benefits that JS frameworks can provide—ease of use, easier learning curve, better documentation and support, regular updates, etc.

This means JS frameworks are, basically, tools to make life easier for you. Pretty much like an artist would use a specific set of colors or brushes simply because those may suit his or her artistic style, a coder may use a given JS framework because it suits his or her coding style and makes life easier.

But the bigger reason is the time and efforts that JS frameworks can save. Ask yourself, what would you prefer: Writing 150 lines of code to accomplish one task, from scratch? Or having a preexisting foundation at your disposal and writing barely 15 lines of code to accomplish the same task with the help of the said foundation? With JS frameworks, programming in itself can become less cumbersome.

Lastly, and this especially applies to you if you are a beginner-level JS developer—frameworks are developed, maintained and curated by JS experts who often know the language and its prowess inside out. This means for newer developers, JS frameworks can serve as handbooks or manuals that can encourage them to write better and cleaner code with efficient calls and arguments.

By ensuring compliance and adherence to coding standards and best practices, JS frameworks can prove as good learning yardsticks. Naturally, efficient and standardized coding practices mean your project consumes less memory, performs faster, has better compatibility with multiple web browsers and operating systems, and so on. There are no poor or incorrectly closed function calls, nor are there arguments that waste system resources and memory.

In fact, for this very reason, many highly experienced JS developers too tend to rely on JS frameworks. Some even go as far as coding their own JS frameworks so as to better utilize system resources and solve a given set of problems as per their requirements.

So, as you can see, using JS frameworks often has more advantages than disadvantages. But in this confusing world of several JS frameworks, which one do you use when?

The bigger names out there are Angular and React. Both are very well known in the field of JS frameworks and each has its own loyal following. Both of these frameworks have chapters dedicated to them in this book, so we would rather not get into the details at this stage.

However, Angular is more apt for building web applications that require just one module framework to play with. React, on the other hand, is more suited as an isomorphic web framework for UI development.

Then, depending on the requirements and needs that your project has, you can opt for a specialized JS framework of your choosing. For instance, if you are working with game engines or 3D scenes, Babylon is the JS framework that you need to be looking at. It combines WebGL with JS to give you the ultimate amazing 3D game engine cum framework.

Similarly, for project and penetration testing, PhantomJS or Karma are ideal picks.

One amazing resource that you can turn to is MicroJS.[1] Basically, this is a "search engine" of sorts for JS frameworks. All you need to do is enter what you "need," say something that is highly mobile-specific or something meant for asynchronous programming. Or even the ability to code your own JS framework!

Thereafter, MicroJS will suggest to you a list of JS frameworks that you can choose from. This can easily help you shortlist and find what you need in an otherwise highly saturated and populous world of JS frameworks.

MicroJS is a handy resource that enlists most of the known smaller JS frameworks and libraries. As a developer, you can make use of it to discover and unravel some cool JS frameworks and libraries and make use of them in your projects!

CONCLUSION

In this chapter, we have covered a good deal of basics related to the JS framework. By now, you should be aware of the following:

- What are JS frameworks?

- How do JS frameworks differ from JS libraries?

- What are the major pros and cons associated with JS frameworks?

- What about framework-less JS?

- Why and when should you consider using JS frameworks and where to find them?

---

[1] See www.microjs.com

Now, since we have innumerable JS frameworks out there, it is not possible to cover every single one of them. In fact, as you read this, there are chances a new JS framework might be released by the time you are done reading this book!

In the chapters that follow, we have put together some of the most useful and versatile JS frameworks for you. Each chapter is devoted to a JS framework and talks about its uses, installation and setup, workflow and methodology, and so on.

Beyond that, we will also attempt to discuss what a given JS framework is best suited for (and what it might not be meant for), so as to help you make a more judicious selection for your web projects.

We will first cover the big three JS frameworks—Angular, React, and VueJS. Thereafter, we will turn our attention to some highly specialized JS frameworks, and then further focus on useful JS tools to help you in your JS development workflow.

The next chapter shall discuss Angular, a very popular JS framework backed by Google. It might be worth noting that you can choose to use your preferred Integrated Development Environment (IDE)/code editor for your projects with JS frameworks.

Depending on your work environment and settings, you might be required to install a series of JS dependencies or libraries. For example, VueJS would require you to have Node.js 8 or higher enabled. For each JS framework, the requirements will be mentioned in the chapter itself.

CHAPTER 2

Getting Started with Node.js

In this chapter, we will be taking a brief look at what Node.js is, what is generally does, and how it can be useful for us. You are free to skip this chapter if you are already familiar with Node and are looking for information directly related to its frameworks only.

WHAT IS NODE.JS?

Node.js—JavaScript code execution environment outside the browser. This platform allows you to write server-side code for dynamic web pages and web applications, as well as for command-line programs. Using Node. js implements the "JavaScript for everything" paradigm. It involves using a single programming language to develop web applications instead of using different languages to work on the frontend and backend. Node.js is a server platform for working with JavaScript through the V8 engine.

It is easier to scale with Node. When thousands of users are connected to the server at the same time, Node works asynchronously, that is, it sets priorities and distributes resources more competently. Java, for example, allocates a separate thread for each connection.

Node.js is well suited for developing RTA web applications that respond to user actions in real time. For example, it can be an online editor like Google Docs, which allows multiple users to work on a single document at the same time.

DOI: 10.1201/9781003203711-2

Node.js easily processes a large number of requests at the same time and ensures the performance of the application. Therefore, server-side JavaScript is often used to create SPA-single-page web applications in which rendering is performed on the client side. Node.js on the backend is used by Netflix, Uber, eBay, Groupon, Yahoo, and other well-known organizations and projects.

Node.js is not an all-purpose platform that will dominate the world of web development. On the contrary, it is a platform for solving strictly defined tasks. It is absolutely necessary to understand this. Of course, you should not use Node.js for operations that load the processor intensively, moreover, the use of Node.js in heavy computing effectively nullifies all of its benefits. Node.js is really good for creating fast, scalable network applications, because it allows you to simultaneously handle a huge number of connections with high bandwidth, which is equivalent to high scalability.

The subtleties of the Node.js "under the hood" is quite interesting. Compared to traditional versions of web services, where each connection (request) generates a new thread, loading the system's RAM and, in the end, parsing this memory without a trace, Node.js is much more economical: It runs in a single thread, uses non-blocking I/O for calls, and supports tens of thousands of competitive connections

WHAT IS JAVASCRIPT?

JavaScript is a multi-paradigm programming language that is commonly used as an embedded tool for programmatically accessing various application objects. From the point of view of web development, without knowledge of this technology, it is impossible to create modern interactive sites. The JS language is what "animates" the page markup (HTML) and user functionality (CMS) of sites. This language allows the page or its individual elements to react to the user's actions. Today, JavaScript is the basic programming language for browsers. It is fully compatible with Windows, Linux, Mac OS operating systems, as well as all popular mobile platforms.

A BRIEF HISTORY

The Node platform.js was introduced in 2009. It was created by engineer Ryan Dahl, and the development was sponsored by Joyent. The company is known for supporting open source projects, including Node.js, Illumos, SmartOS.

Ryan Dahl used to create Node.js engine V8. The platform is implemented with a low-level non-blocking I/O model, which is built on an event-oriented model.

At the end of 2014, engineer Fedor Indutny, who was part of the main development team of the platform, created a popular fork of Node.js— io.js. The fork appeared due to the dissatisfaction of the developers with the policy of the company Joyent.

Platform io.js superior to Node.js in performance. But the creators of the fork decided to reunite with Node in 2015.js to influence the development of the main platform. Currently, the development is formally managed by Node.js Foundation.

WHY SHOULD WE LEARN NODE.JS?

The market has witnessed the acquisition of several Node pioneers.js, including StrongLoop by IBM, FeedHenry by Red Hat, and Modulus by Progress Software.

Experts in the IT industry note that a JavaScript-based scripting language is a must-have tool for developing and delivering applications in modern companies.

Node.js continues to evolve at an almost unprecedented rate. Over the past 5 years, developers have added more than 190,000 modules to Node.js (and other JavaScript libraries). This exceeds the entire Perl CPAN repository that has been compiled for 20 years, and bypasses Java Maven Central, despite a smaller number of developers Node.js.

What was the reason for such popularity among enterprise developers, and can CIOs be sure that Node.will js be actively used for at least 10 years?

The Node.js module support ecosystem around the core has experienced strong growth. The Node community has benefited greatly from the existence of the Node Package Manager (NPM), which provides a central repository of shared modules.

This is a key part of a flexible and easy way to work with Node.js. It allows each application to have the necessary modules in its own dependency tree. Thus, each application can have its own set of modules, which avoids dependency conflicts with other applications.

This is a flexible tool based on Node.js using the service npmjs.org, led to a significant increase in the number of common modules and to the fact that npmjs.org it became a repository not only for the server Node.js, but also for client-side JavaScript modules.

At an early stage of Node development.js has been used by companies such as Netflix, Walmart, PayPal, Dow Jones, and Groupon. They created internal teams that used Node, taking a divide-and-conquer approach: Breaking down what used to be more of a "monolithic" approach to building web services. This allowed them to quickly develop and update solutions for various business areas and immediately deploy microservices in production.

NODE.JS BECOMES MAINSTREAM

Node.js is especially well suited for companies that have a web infrastructure and mobile applications, in the backend of which it is necessary to quickly introduce innovations using an architecture built on microservices. This includes organizations that may seem conservative, but are faced with the need to develop applications that meet the rapid changes in the business world, while maintaining the stability and security of existing systems.

These double demands have forced IT teams to change the way they think. Almost all companies had to find ways to quickly respond to requests for business software, while maintaining the current legacy code, which changes significantly less often. Node.js is one of the tools for teams developing interaction systems, such as mobile solutions.

Node.js is often praised for responding to corporate requests and allowing you to build applications with an API that can access the backend and large amounts of data in an easy and efficient manner. Indeed, the focus on the reused RESTful API as a more flexible way to build the architecture of large-scale software systems allowed Node.js find your place.

Node.js is able to significantly reduce the application development time while maintaining the same functionality. John K. Ousterhout, who helped develop the significant Tcl/Tk scripting language and toolset, argued back in the 1990s that scripting programming languages are inherently more productive than heavier programming languages like C or C++.

Compared to heavier stacks, application development with Node.js is faster, and with the development of the Node ecosystem, it only accelerates. This is the case when it is worth spending time searching for what is already in the Node community, and finding out whether it is possible to reuse some of the common modules.

In the development environment, Node is treated very favorably and respected by specialists in this technology. The unity of developers and their morale is raised if there is a team working with Node.js in the IT structure of the organization. This is perceived as an interesting and really cool opportunity.

Node.js is great for applications built on a microservice architecture, thanks to its low CPU consumption, its processing power, and efficient use of RAM. This advantage is especially evident for tasks that involve I/O operations rather than CPU usage, since the implementation of the Node.js execution model allows you to use "light" parallelism, based on a single thread of execution model, which does not require complex parallel programming techniques.

By combining all of this—the mindset of programmers and the various technical advantages of a lightweight approach-companies get a new approach to solving IT problems with a development team that is motivated to solve them and armed with a high-speed set of tools.

WHAT WAS NODE.JS CREATED FOR?

Node.js is not a separate programming language, but a platform for using JavaScript on the server side. If we talk about the language, then both the frontend and the backend use the same JavaScript. The only difference is in the set of APIs that frontenders and backenders use.

Browser-based JavaScript uses Web APIs that provide access to the DOM and user interface of pages and web applications. Server-side JavaScript uses APIs that provide access to the application file system, http requests, and streams.

That is, Node.js is a technology for using JS on the backend. The features and prospects of the development of the JavaScript language can be found in the corresponding article, and here we are talking about one of the technologies of this language.

One of the most difficult problems when writing systems that communicate over a network is processing input and output. Read and write data to and from the network, to disk, and other devices. Moving data takes time, and properly planning these actions can greatly affect the system response time for the user or network requests.

In the traditional method of processing input and output, it is assumed that a function, for example, ReadFile, starts reading a file and stops working only when the file is fully read. This is called synchronous I/O (input/ output).

Node was conceived to facilitate and simplify the use of asynchronous I/O.

JavaScript code easily fits into a Node-type system. It is one of the few languages that does not have an I/O system built in. Therefore, JavaScript is easily embedded in a rather eccentric approach to I/O in Node and as a result does not generate two different input and output systems. In 2009, when developing Node, people were already using callback-based I/O in the browser, so the community around the language was used to the asynchronous programming style.

MAIN FEATURES OF NODE.JS

Let's look at the main features of Node.js.

Speed

One of the main attractive features of Node.js is the speed. JavaScript code that runs in the Node.js environment can be twice as fast as code written in compiled languages like C or Java, and orders of magnitude faster than interpreted languages like Python or Ruby. The reason for this is the non-blocking architecture of the platform, and the specific results depend on the performance tests used, but, in general, Node.js is a very fast platform.

Simplicity

The Node.js platform is easy to learn and use. In fact, it is quite simple, especially when compared to some other server platforms.

JavaScript

In the Node.js environment executes code written in JavaScript. This means that millions of frontend developers who already use JavaScript in the browser can write both server-side and client-side code in the same programming language without having to learn a completely new tool to move to server-side development. The browser and the server use the same language concepts. Also, in Node.js can quickly switch to using the new ECMAScript standards as they are implemented on the platform. To do this, you don't need to wait until users update their browsers, since Node.js is a server environment that is fully controlled by the developer. As a result, new language features are available when you install a version of Node.js that supports them.

V8 Engine

At the heart of Node.js, among other solutions, is the open-source JavaScript engine V8 from Google, used in Google Chrome and other browsers. This means that Node.js uses the work of thousands of engineers who have made the Chrome JavaScript runtime incredibly fast and continue to work towards improving V8.

Asynchrony

In traditional programming languages (C, Java, Python, PHP) all instructions, by default, are blocking, unless the developer explicitly takes care of asynchronous code execution. As a result, if in such an environment, make a network request to download a certain JSON code, the execution of the thread from which the request is made will be suspended until the response is received and processed. JavaScript makes it much easier to write asynchronous and non-blocking code using a single thread, callback functions, and an event-driven development approach. Every time we need to perform a heavy operation, we pass a callback to the appropriate mechanism, which will be called immediately after the completion of this operation. As a result, you don't need to wait for the results of such operations to continue working. A similar mechanism has emerged in browsers. We can't afford to wait for, say, the end of an AJAX request, without being able to respond to user actions, such as button clicks. In order for users to be comfortable working with web pages, everything, both loading data from the network and processing button clicks, must occur simultaneously, in real time. If you have ever created a button click event handler, you have already used asynchronous programming techniques.

Asynchronous mechanisms allow a single Node.js server handle thousands of connections at the same time, without loading the programmer with tasks for managing threads and organizing parallel code execution. Such things are often sources of error. Node.js provides the developer with non-blocking basic I/O mechanisms, and, in general, libraries used in the Node.js environment, written using non-blocking paradigms. This makes blocking code behavior the exception rather than the norm.

When Node.js needs to perform an I/O operation, such as loading data from the network, accessing a database, or accessing a file system, instead of blocking the main thread, Node.js, from waiting for the results of such an operation initiates its execution and continues to do other things until the results of this operation are received.

Libraries

Thanks to the simplicity and convenience of working with the package manager for Node.js, which is called npm, the Node.js ecosystem is downright thriving. Now the npm registry has more than half a million open source packages that any Node.js can freely use developer. Having considered some of the main features of the Node.js platform, let's try it out in action. Let's start with the installation.

BEST USE CASES

Let's discuss some reasons to explore Node.js:

1. **Real-time applications:** Users want to interact with each other in real time. Chat, games, constant social media updates, collaboration tools, e-commerce websites, real-time tracking apps, the marketplace-each of these features requires real-time communication between users, clients, and servers over the Internet. Building a real-time application is challenging because it happens on a massive scale, supporting hundreds, thousands, and even millions of users. Real-time communication between the client and the server requires fast and constant I/O.

   Node.js is best suited for such applications. The synchronization process with Node.js is fast and organized, as events control the architecture that serves both the client and server sides. The event loop via the web socket protocol handles the multi-user function. It works in TCP and avoids HTTP congestion. Node.js also makes RTA lightweight, scalable, maintainable, and user-friendly in terms of software development.

2. **Low learning curve:** No matter what language you use for the backend, you'll still need JavaScript for the frontend, so instead of spending time learning a server-side language like Php, Java, or Ruby on Rails, you can spend all your effort learning and mastering JS in it. Javascript of the same language can be used both on the client side and on the server side. Thus, a developer who knows JS can act as a full-stack developer without learning additional languages. The interface and backend are also easier to keep in sync due to the unified use of the language on both sides.

For startups, this is one of the big benefits of getting their work done quickly with fewer developers. There is no need to divide the team into two sides. This provides better performance and the ability to share or re-process code, and within the team ensures a smooth exchange of knowledge.

3. **Performance and scalability:** Node.js is built on Google's Chrome V8 engine. This allows Node to provide a server-side runtime environment that compiles and executes JavaScript at lightning speed. The V8 engine compiles JavaScript into machine code, instead of interpreting it or executing it as byte code, and this makes Node really fast. Lightweight Javascript achieves high performance with fewer lines of code compared to Java or C. The Chrome V8 engine is also constantly being updated as Google continues to invest heavily in it.

The reason for fast Javascript execution is the Event Loop. In a typical application server model that uses blocking I/O—in this case, the application must process each request sequentially, suspending the threads until they are processed. This can complicate the application and, of course, slow down the application.

Node.js supports an event loop that manages all asynchronous operations for you. This allows you to use non-blocking I/O, in which threads (in this case sequential, not parallel), can manage multiple requests. If it cannot be processed, it is actually "held" as a promise, meaning that it can be executed later without delaying other threads. This whole process allows developers to manage more operations using less memory and resources.

Paypal, which used Node in its app, found that the app was created twice as fast with fewer people, 33% fewer lines of code, and 40% fewer files. More importantly, they doubled the number of requests processed per second and reduced the average response time by 35%. As such, Node is a great choice for building highly scalable applications.

4. **NPM support with rich modules:** Only a few programming languages offer a rich ecosystem of packages, like Node.js. When you install Node.js, it automatically installs NPM programs. Any Node developer.js can package its libraries and solutions into a module that anyone can install using the official Node package manager, NPM. Thousands of Javascript development libraries and tools are built on

NPM. With the continued support of the Node.js community, NPM focuses on encouraging users to add new packages so that you have a variety of ready-made solutions for a specific problem.

To date, it has more than 60,000 modules, and it continues to grow every day. Isn't it worth using these modules for some common functions instead of writing code from scratch? This great feature of Node: reduces complexity, makes development easier, faster, and allows you to easily share, update, and even reuse code.

5. **A useful unified code base:** Using the node, it is easy to send and synchronize data between the server and client encoding. By using the same Javascript language on both sides, your source code will be cleaner and more consistent. You will use the same naming convention, the same tools, and the same best practices. Developers' time is saved to a greater extent thanks to this feature.

6. **Data streaming:** Like an array in data structures, streams are a set of data, and processing this data requires first-class input/output data processing techniques. Node.js comes to the rescue because it handles the kind of I/O process that allows users to simultaneously transcode media files while they are downloading. This takes less time compared to other data processing methods to process the data. Node.js threads greatly simplifies I/O tasks.

There are four types of threads used by Node.js—Writable, Readable, Duplex, and Transform, as well as the Pipe method for processing data. Developers can take amazing advantage of shaping features such as processing files when they are uploaded. Node.js threads allow applications to consume less memory while simultaneously working with large amounts of data to run faster. This feature gives more advantages to a developer working in real-time with audio or video encoding.

7. **Well suited for creating microservices:** As we have already said, Node.js is highly scalable and lightweight, so it is a favorite for microservice architectures. In a nutshell, microservice architectures mean splitting an application into isolated and independent services. This makes it easier to update and maintain the architecture, since your services are separate from each other, and you can add

new or fix existing architecture without affecting other parts of the applications. Node.js is well suited for designing such architectures with Node modules, which are the building blocks of Node.js functions. Thanks to this architecture, applications can be developed, processed, operated and tested independently, which saves you from infrastructure risks. This feature provides the ability to reuse code between the client and server sides, and also reduces development time and cost, since you only need to consider what new services have been introduced or updated.

8. **Strong corporate support:** In 2015, a number of companies, including IBM, Microsoft, PayPal, Fidelity, SAP, organized the Node.js Foundation. It is an independent community that aims to promote the development of the core Node.js tools. The Node.js Foundation was created to accelerate the development of Node.js, and it was intended to ensure its wide distribution. There is a continuous growth of organizations that use Node.js in production. It includes almost three hundred well-known companies, such as Medium, Uber.

Let's look at real-world examples in which the use of Node.js would be the perfect solution.

API Above the Object Database

Although Node.js is especially good in the context of real-time applications, and it is also quite suitable for providing information from object databases (e.g., MongoDB). The data stored in JSON format allows Node.js function without loss of match and without data transformation.

For example, if you use Rails, you would have to convert JSON to binary models, and then provide them again as JSON over HTTP when the data is consumed by Backbone.js, Angular.js or even regular jQuery AJAX calls. Working with Node.js, you can simply provide your JSON objects to the client via the REST API, so that the client consumes them. Also, you don't have to worry about converting between JSON and anything else when reading the database and writing to it (if you use MongoDB). So, you do without a lot of transformations, using a universal data serialization format that is used both on the client, on the server, and in the database.

Chat

Chat is the most typical real-time multi-user application. From IRC (there were times), using a variety of open and open protocols, operating through non-standard ports, we have come to the present, when everything can be implemented on the Node.js using web sockets operating over the standard port 80.

The chat program is really an ideal product for using Node.js: This is a lightweight, high-traffic, data-intensive (but almost non-computationally intensive) application running on a variety of distributed devices. In addition, it is very convenient to learn from it, since for all its simplicity, it covers most of the paradigms that you may need to use in a typical application Node.js.

Let's try to figure out how it works.

In the simplest case, we have a single chat room on our site, where users come and exchange messages in the "one—to-many" mode (in fact, "to all"). Let's say we have three visitors on our site, and all of them can write messages on our forum.

On the server side, we have a simple Express application.js, which implements two things: (1) a GET "/" request handler that serves a web page that contains both a message forum and a "Send" button that initializes a new entered message, and (2) a web socket server that listens for new messages issued by web socket clients.

On the client side, we have an HTML page that has two handlers configured: one of them listens for click events on the "Send" button, which picks up the entered message and sends it to the web socket, and the other listens for new incoming messages on the client to serve the web sockets (i.e., messages sent by other clients that the server is going to display using this special client).

Here's what happens when one of the clients sends a message:

The browser picks up a click on the "Send" button using a JavaScript handler, takes the value from the input field (i.e., the message text), and outputs a web socket message using a web socket client connected to our server (this client is initialized along with the web page).

The server component of the web socket connection receives the message and forwards it to all other connected clients using the broadcast method.

All clients receive a new push message using a web socket component running on a web page. Then they pick up the content of the message and update the web page, adding a new post to the forum.

This is the simplest example. For a more reliable solution, you can use a simple cache based on Redis storage. An even more advanced solution is a message queue, which allows you to handle message routing to clients and provides a more reliable delivery mechanism that allows you to compensate for temporary connection interruptions or store messages for registered clients while they are offline. But no matter what optimizations you perform, Node.js will still operate according to the same basic principles: react to events, handle multiple competitive connections, and maintain smooth user interactions.

Input Queues

If you get large amounts of competitive data, then the database can become a bottleneck. As shown above, Node.js easily handles competitive connections as such. But since accessing the database is a blocking operation (in this case), we have problems. The solution is to capture the behavior of the client before the data is actually written to the database.

When using this approach, the responsiveness of the system is maintained even under high load, which is especially useful if the client does not need confirmation that the data recording was successful. Typical examples: Logging or recording user activity data (user tracking), processed in batches and not used later; operations that should be reflected instantly (for example, updating the number of "likes" on Facebook), where consistency is acceptable in the end, so often used in the NoSQL world.

Data is queued using a special infrastructure for caching and working with message queues (for example, RabbitMQ, ZeroMQ) and digested by a separate database process designed for batch writing, or by special database interface services designed for intensive calculations. Similar behavior can be implemented using other languages/frameworks, but on different hardware and not with such high and stable bandwidth.

In short, Node allows you to postpone write operations to the database until later, continuing to work in the same mode as if these writes were completed successfully.

Data Streaming

On more traditional web platforms, HTTP requests and responses are treated as isolated events; but they are actually streams. This point can be used in Node.js to create some cool features. For example, you can process files while they are still being uploaded, because the data comes in a stream, and we can work with them online. This can be done, for example, when encoding video or audio in real time, as well as when installing a proxy between different data sources (for more information, see the next section).

Proxy

Node.js can be used as a server proxy, and in this case it can handle a large number of simultaneous connections in non-blocking mode. This is especially useful when mediating between different services that have different response times, or when collecting data from multiple sources.

For example, let's consider a server application that exchanges information with third-party resources, collects information from various sources, or stores resources such as images and videos, which are then provided to third-party cloud services.

Although there are dedicated proxy servers, it is convenient to use Node instead, especially if the proxy infrastructure does not exist, or if you need a solution for local development. Here I mean that it is possible to create a client application where the Node development server will be applied. js, where we will store resources and make proxies/stubs for API requests, and in real conditions such interactions will already be performed using a dedicated proxy service (nginx, HAProxy, etc.)

Dashboard for App Monitoring

This is another practical case for which the "Node+Web Sockets" model is ideal. Here we track site visitors and visualize their interactions in real time (if you are interested in such an idea, it is already being solved with the help of Hummingbird).

You can collect statistics about the user in real time and even go to a higher level by adding targeted interactions with the user, opening a communication channel as soon as the guest reaches a specific point in your funnel (if you are interested in such an idea, it is already solved using CANDDi).

Imagine how you could optimize your business if you could find out in real time what your users are doing—as well as visualize their interactions. Bidirectional Node sockets.js opens up such an opportunity for you.

Informational Panel for System Tracking

Now let's talk about the infrastructure aspects. Let's say there is a SaaS provider that wants to offer users a page for tracking services (say, a GitHub status page). Having a Node event loop.js, you can create a powerful web interface where service states will be asynchronously checked in real time, and data will be sent to the client via web sockets.

This technology allows you to report on the status of both internal (intra-corporate) and public services in real time. Let's develop this idea a bit and try to imagine a network operations center (NOC) that monitors the operation of applications of a telecom operator, cloud service provider/ hosting provider, or some financial organization. All this works in an open web stack based on Node.js and web sockets, not Java and/or Java applets.

Stock Trader Dashboard

Let's go back to the application layer. Another segment where PC software dominates, but they can easily be replaced by a web-based solution that works in real time is software for stock trading, where quotes are tracked, calculations and technical analysis are performed, graphs and charts are drawn.

If you use a real-time web solution in this case, the broker using it will be able to easily switch between workstations or locations.

WHAT JAVASCRIPT KNOWLEDGE YOU NEED TO HAVE TO START LEARNING NODE.JS?

Let's imagine that you have just started programming. How deep you need to learn JavaScript to successfully master Node.js? It is difficult for a beginner to reach a level where he will gain sufficient confidence in his professional skills. In addition, while studying programming, you may feel that you do not understand exactly where browser-based JavaScript ends and development begins for Node.js. If you are at the very beginning of the path of JavaScript programming, before writing for Node.js, well master the following language concepts: Lexical constructions, Expressions, Types, Variables, Functions, Arrow functions, Cycles, Scopes, Arrays, Template strings, Working in strict mode.

In fact, this list goes on, but if you master all this, it means that you will lay a good foundation for productive client and server development in JavaScript.

WHICH FAMOUS COMPANIES USE NODE.JS?

Given the long list of benefits of using Node.js, it's easy to believe that the list of large companies using this technology, includes NASA, Uber, and Twitter. Who uses Node.js, why they chose to switch to Node.js and how did it turn out for them?

NASA

NASA is one of the most famous organizations in the world. NASA decided to switch to Node.js after an incident that nearly resulted in fatal consequences. The reason for the incident was a long access time due to inefficient data storage between multiple points. NASA developers felt it was important to move the data to a cloud database to reduce access time. In addition, most of NASA's applications were written in JavaScript.

Trello

Trello is a project management tool used in a variety of industries and countries. Such a platform requires instant updates in real time and without delays, that is why Trello has become one of the companies using Node. js on the server side. Trello needs to manage multiple real-time server connections to ensure that updates are delivered smoothly and on time.

LinkedIn

One more company using Node.js is LinkedIn, the largest social platform for business and employment. Its popularity continues to grow rapidly from year to year. After switching from Ruby on Rails to Node.js company has created an application that works ten times faster than the old version. The decision was made due to the synchronization of the application in Ruby, which led to an increase in loading time, especially with an increase in traffic.

Twitter

Over than 80% of Twitter account owners access them via a smartphone. So the company decided to create Twitter Lite—an application with minimal functionality, able to work even with a poor Internet connection. In addition, the website version of Twitter was not optimized for poor connection conditions. All this has led to the fact that Twitter has become one of the companies that use Node.js.

INSTALLATION AND SET UP

Installing the Node software platform.js, in order to give JavaScript the ability to interact with I/O devices through its API and connect various external libraries.

Installing Node.js on Windows

First, you need to install the correct console for WIndows.

After that, you can proceed to the installation Node.js. For Windows, there is only one way.

You need to go to the official website https://nodejs.org and on the main page, download the latest stable version.

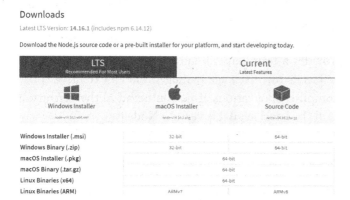

After downloading, the installer should run and install Node.js, just like any other program.

Let's make sure everything is settled. To do this, check the Node version in cmder.js using the command:

node-v and *npm-v*

Installing Node.js on OS X

Go to the site https://nodejs.org and on the main page, download the latest stable version by clicking on the corresponding button.

Node.js® is a JavaScript runtime built on Chrome's V8 JavaScript engine. Node.js uses an event-driven, non-blocking I/O model that makes it lightweight and efficient. Node.js' package ecosystem, npm, is the largest ecosystem of open source libraries in the world.

Important security notification regarding npm

Download for OS X (x64)

Other Downloads | Changelog | API Docs   Other Downloads | Changelog | API Docs

Or have a look at the LTS schedule.

After downloading, it is enough to install the package through the installer and you can start using it.

Installing Node.js Via the Package Manager

Android

Android support is still experimental in Node.js, so the precompiled binaries are not yet publicly available.

However, there are also third-party solutions. For example, the Termux community provides a terminal emulator and a Linux environment for Android, as well as its own package manager and an extensive collection of many pre-compiled applications. This command in the Termux application will install the latest available version Node.js:

```
pkg install nodejs
```

nvm

Node Version Manager is a bash script used to manage multiple released versions Node.js. It allows you to perform operations such as installing, deleting, switching versions, etc. To install nvm, use this installation script.

On Unix/OS X Node systems.js created from source code can be installed using nvm by installing in the default nvm folder:

```
env VERSION='python tools/getnodeversion.py' make
install DESTDIR='nvm_version_path v$VERSION' PREFIX=""
```

After that, you can use nvm to switch between released versions and versions built from source. For example, if the Node version.js v8.0.0-pre:

```
nvm use 8
```

MacOS

Just download the macOS installer directly from the website nodejs.org.

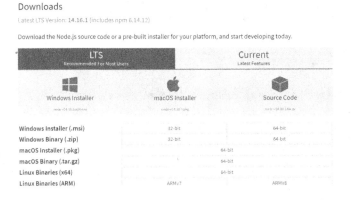

Downloads

Latest LTS Version: 14.16.1 (includes npm 6.14.12)

Download the Node.js source code or a pre-built installer for your platform, and start developing today.

	LTS Recommended For Most Users		Current Latest Features
	Windows Installer	macOS Installer	Source Code
	node-v14.16.0x64.msi	node-v14.16.1.pkg	node-v14.16.1.tar.gz
Windows Installer (.msi)	32-bit		64-bit
Windows Binary (.zip)	32-bit		64-bit
macOS Installer (.pkg)		64-bit	
macOS Binary (.tar.gz)		64-bit	
Linux Binaries (x64)		64-bit	
Linux Binaries (ARM)		ARMv7	ARMv8

If you want to download a package from bash:

```
curl "https://nodejs.org/dist/latest/node-${VERSION:-
$(wget -qO- https://nodejs.org/dist/latest/ | sed -nE
's|.*>node-(.*)\.pkg</a>.*|\1|p')}.pkg" > "$HOME/
Downloads/node-latest.pkg" && sudo installer -store
-pkg "$HOME/Downloads/node-latest.pkg" -target "/"
```

Arch Linux

Node packages.js and npm are available in the community repository.

```
pacman -S nodejs npm
```

After installation, you have a new command in the "node" command line. You can use Node in two ways.

The first one is without arguments: this command opens an interactive mode on the command line where you can execute JavaScript code.$node > console. log ('Hello World'); Hello World undefined.

In this example, I just typed "console. log ('Hello World');" and hit Enter. Node will start executing and we will see our message. It will also write "undefined," because it prints the return value, and console.log returns nothing. Another way to use Node.js is the creation of a Javascript file.

So, let's create a file:

```
console.log('Hello World');
```

And save it to the directory from which we will run this file. To go to the command line, just write cd full_name_of_directory (or you can use relative addressing).

Run in the command line:

```
$ node hello.js
Hello World
```

In this case, we moved the message of the console.log file and sent this file to the node command as an argument. Node runs the JavaScript code in the file and prints out 'Hello World.'

I/O Files With Node.js

Running clean JavaScript is great, but not very useful. So in Node.js has a huge number of libraries (modules) to do real things. In this example, we will open a file with records and process it.

example_log.txt

2021-09-09T10:15:33.166Z A 8

2021-09-09T10:16:33.166Z B 8

2021-09-09T10:17:33.166Z C 7

2021-09-09T10:18:33.166Z C 7

2021-09-09T10:19:33.166Z A 8

What this file means is not so important, but you need to know that each record contains a date, a letter, and a value. We want to correlate each letter with its corresponding value and read the contents of the file.

my_parser.js

```
// Loading the file system module
var fs = require('fs');

// Reading the contents of the file into memory
fs. ReadFile('example_file.txt', function (err,
LogData) {

// If an error occurs, we throw an exception
// and the program ends with
if (err) throw err;

// LogData is an object of the Buffer type, translated
// into a string
var text = logData.toString();
});
```

Fortunately, Node.js greatly facilitates the processing of file contents with the built-in filesystem (fs) module. The fs module has a ReadFile function that takes the path to the file and a callback. The callback will be executed when the file is fully read. The file data comes in the form of a Buffer type, which is a set of bits. We can convert to a string using the toString function().

Now let's add the parser (it is written in clean JavaScript).

my_parser.js
```
// loading the file system (fs) module)
```

```
var fs = require ('fs');
// reading the contents of the file into memory
fs. ReadFile('example_file.txt', function (err,
LogData) {

// If an error occurs, we throw an exception
// and the program ends
if (err) throw err;

// LogData has the Buffer type, convert to a string
var text = LogData.toString ();
var
results = {};

// Splitting the text into an array of lines
var lines = text.split('\n');

lines. forEach (function (string) {
var parts = line.split('. ');
var letter = parts[1];
var count = parseInt(parts[2]);

if (! results[letter]) {
results[letter] = 0;
}

results[letter] += parseInt(count);
});

console. log (results);
/ / { A: 2, B: 1, C: 14 }
});
```

When the file is an argument to the node command, the result is printed and output is performed.

```
$ node my_parser.js
{ A: 2, B: 1, C: 14 }
```

Asynchronous Calls in Node.js

As you noticed in the last example, for Node.js is characterized by the use of asynchronous calls. Essentially, you write what needs to be done, and when it's done, a callback will be called, because node.js is single-threaded. While you are waiting for the callback to start, Node.js can go away and do other things instead of blocking until the request is completed.

This is especially important for web servers. It is quite common for modern web applications to have access to databases. While you wait for the result to return from the database, Node can handle more requests. This allows you to handle thousands of concurrent requests with little overhead compared to creating a separate thread for each connection.

NODE.JS FOR SERVER APPLICATION DEVELOPMENT

TheNode.js is based on asynchrony. In addition to non-blocking I/O, this allows the server application to run on a Node.js serves many more client requests per unit of time than a similar application developed on most other server development technologies.

What does this mean for business?

- You can run your project with relatively little cost for the server infrastructure.

- With a well-built architecture, this allows you to scale your business without investing a lot of money.

What does this mean for developers?

- If you do not have an understanding of how asynchronous code works and experience with it, then it will be very difficult at first. It is difficult to understand that some instruction written "upstream" may be executed much later than the subsequent ones, or it may not be executed at all. You will need to thoroughly study the concepts of callbacks, promises, async-await wrappers over promises, synchronous and asynchronous generators, and iterators. But it is very well-structured thinking, allows you to take a different look at the process of executing the program and understand how much time a "normal"—synchronous-program wastes during waiting periods, as well as learn how to save this time.

- A good understanding of asynchronous approaches to development greatly increases the value of a specialist in the labor market and, accordingly, allows you to claim a higher salary.

Node allows you to quickly develop an MVP. Node has already developed a large number of packages with different functionality. You cannot spend

time on the development of the basic functionality, and immediately focus on the business logic.
What does this mean for business?

- The new product will be brought to market faster (TTM will be reduced).

- Less money will be spent on the development process, because it will take less developer hours to create the first version of the product.

- The hypotheses formed during the initial market research will be tested faster, adjustments to the product will be made faster, and funds will eventually be turned around faster. This is a very important characteristic for project investors.

What does this mean for developers?

- You don't have to invent new things on each project, which inevitably causes a lot of errors and makes the work boring, but deal closely with the tasks that are important for the project.

- Greater freedom in choosing the approach, building the architecture, and finalizing the standard functionality that does not meet the requirements of the architect and/or the customer.

- Node is built on the basis of the JavaScript language. As a result, this significantly increases the likelihood of developing full-stack specialists in the development team: Frontenders who are well versed in the backend or backenders who are well versed in the frontend.

Node.js is very closely related to JavaScript, the syntax and architectural approaches are identical, only the "bindings" (browser and server) differ.
What does this mean for business?

- The development team will have specialists with a broader view of the problem, which means that the burden on management will be reduced.

- The development process will be more efficient, because it is always easier and faster for a person (a full-stack developer) to negotiate with himself than with another person. Thus, the costs of communication between specialists are reduced.

- During the development process, there will be fewer errors, since floating bugs often occur at the junction of different development technologies with different types of data.

What does this mean for developers?

- If you previously had to work closely with the frontend, then there is a good understanding of the processes that occur with the data in the user part of the resource, and, as a result, a simpler dialogue with the frontenders.

- A good fullstack specialist is often more appreciated in the market than a good backend or frontend developer.

- If you have a sufficient amount of time allocated for the development of the project, you can independently make both the front and back, thereby avoiding a huge number of "collisions," which often take a lot of time to solve.

CREATING A WEB SERVER USING NODE.JS

As already mentioned, Node can't do anything by itself. One of the built-in modules makes it easy to create a simple HTTP server, an example of its use is given on the main page of the official site.

mywebserver.js

```
var http = require('http');

http.createServer(function (req, res) {
    res.writeHead(200, {'Content-Type': 'text/plain'});
    res.end('Hello World\n');
}).listen(8080);

console.log('Hello World');
```

One more time: This is a basic web server, not a server with full functionality. It can't serve images or HTML files. In fact, whatever request you send will return "Hello World." However, you can run this script, go to http://localhost:8080 in your browser and see this text.

```
$ node mywebserver.js
```

You may have already noticed that your application is on node.js doesn't stop anymore. This is because you have created a web server, and your application is on node.js responds to requests until you stop it yourself.

If you want to make a web server with full functionality, you will have to do some work: you will need to check all the requests, read the appropriate files, and send the output back. There is also good news. People have already done this hard work for you.

In this chapter, we have covered the basics related to Node.js We now have a fair idea of what Node.js is, what Node is capable of, and how we can compile some basic tasks using it. In the next chapter, we will dive deeper into the world of Node.

CHAPTER 3

Doing More with Node.js

In the previous chapter, we covered some basics related to Node, such as installation, creating a basic and simple web server, and more. In this chapter, we will now turn our attention to more refined details and extensibility of Node. First up, let us focus on Node Modules—a key component of the Node.js ecosystem.

MODULES

Aside from the few variables mentioned, such as the console and the process, the node has little functionality in the global scope. To access the rest of the built-in functions, you need to access the module system.

The CommonJS system is built into the Node and is used to load everything from the built-in modules and downloaded libraries to the files that are part of your program.

When calling require Node, you must convert the specified string to a file name. Paths starting with "/", "./", or "../" are converted to paths relative to the current one. "./"means the current directory, ".. /" means the directory above, and "/" means the root directory of the file system. If you request it "./ world/world" from the file /home/marijn/elife/run.js, The node will try to download the file/home/marijn/elife/world/world.js. Expansion.js can be omitted.

When a string that does not look like a relative or absolute path is passed, it is assumed that it is either a built-in module, or a module installed in the node_modules directory. For example, require ("fs") will give you a built-in module for working with the file system, and require ("elife") will try to load the library from node_modules/elife/. A typical method of installing libraries is using NPM (Node Package Manager), which we'll return to later.

To demonstrate, let's make a simple project from two files. The first one is called main.js, and it will define a script called from the command line, designed to distort strings.

```
var garble = require("./garble");
// Index 2 contains the first argument of the program
from the command line
var argument = process.argv[2];
console.log(garble(argument));
```

The garble.js file defines a string distortion library that can be used both by a previously defined command-line program and by other scripts that need direct access to the garble function.

```
module.exports = function(string) { return string.
split("").map(function(ch) { return String.
fromCharCode(ch.charCodeAt(0) + 5); }).join(""); };
```

Replacing module.exports instead of adding properties to it allows us to export a specific value from the module. In this case, the result of our module's request will be the distortion function itself.

The function splits the string into characters using split with an empty string, and then replaces all the characters with others whose codes are 5 units larger. It then joins the result back into a string.

Now we can call our tool:

```
node main.js JavaScript
Orrasjhdsfgsdjfgsd
```

HTTP Module

Another main module is "http." It provides functionality for creating HTTP servers and HTTP requests. Here's everything you need to run a simple HTTP server:

```
var http = require("http");
var server = http.createServer(function(request,
response) {
response.writeHead(200, {"Content-Type": "text/html"});
```

```
response.write("<h1>Hi!</h1><p>You requested <code> "+
request. url + " </code>< / p>");
response.end();
});
server.listen(8000);
```

By running the script on your machine, you can guide the browser to the address localhost:8000/hello, in that way creating a request to the server. It will respond with a small HTML page.

The function passed as an argument to createserver is called every time a connection to the server is attempted. The request and response variables are objects that represent input and output data. The first one contains information about the request, for example, the url property contains the request URL.

To send something back, use the methods of the response object. The first, writeHead, writes the response headers (see Chapter 17). You give it a status code (in this case 200 for "OK") and an object containing the header values. Here we tell the client that it should wait for the HTML document.

Thereafter comes the response body (the document itself), sent via *response.write*. You can call this method multiple times if you want to send the response in chunks. For example, passing the streaming data as it arrives. Finally, *response.end* signals the end of the response.

Calling server.listen causes the server to listen for requests on port 8000. Therefore, you need to go to localhost:8000 in the browser, and not just to localhost (where the default port is 80).

To stop such a Node script, which does not terminate automatically because it is waiting for the following events (in this case, connections), press Ctrl-C.

A real web server does much more than what is described in the example. It looks at the request method (the method property) to understand what action the client is trying to perform, and at the request URL to understand on which resource this action should be performed. Next, you will see a more advanced version of the server.

To create an HTTP client, we can use the "http" request module function.

```
var http = require("http");
var request = http.request({
hostname: "eloquentjavascript.net",
path: "/20_node.html",
```

```
method: "GET",
headers: {Accept: "text/html"}
}, function(response) {
console. log ("Service responded with a code",
response. statusCode);
});
request.end();
```

The first argument of request configures the request, explaining to Node which server we will communicate with, which path the request will have and which method to use. The second is a function, which will need to be called at the end of the request. The response object is passed to it, which contains all the information about the response—for example, the status code.

Like the server's response object, the object returned by request allows you to pass data by the write method and end the request by the end method. The example does not use write, because GET requests should not contain data in the body.

For requests to secure URLs (HTTPS), Node offers the https module, which has its own request function, similar to *http.request*.

Streams

We saw two examples of threads in the HTTP examples—a response object that the server can write to, and a request object that is returned from http.request

Write-only streams are a popular concept in Node interfaces. All threads have a write method that can be given a string or a Buffer object.

The end method closes the stream, and if there is an argument, it outputs a piece of data before closing it. Both methods can be given a callback function via an additional argument, which they will call at the end of the write or the end of the stream.

It is possible to create a stream pointing to a file using the fs.createWriteStream function. After that, you can use the write method to write to the file in chunks, rather than the whole file, as in fs.WriteFile.

Read-only streams will be a little more complicated. Both the request variable passed to the function for the callback to the HTTP server and the response variable passed to the HTTP client are read-only streams. (The server reads the request and then writes the responses, and the client writes the request first and then reads the response). Reading from a stream is done through event handlers, not through methods.

Objects that create events in Node have an on method, similar to the browser's addEventListener method. You give it an event name and a function, and it registers this function so that it is called immediately when the event occurs.

Read-only threads have "data" and "end" events. The first occurs when the data is received, the second-at the end. This model is suitable for streaming data that can be processed instantly, even if not the entire document is received. The file can be read as a stream via fs.createReadStream.

The following code creates a server that reads the request bodies and sends them in response in a stream of uppercase text.

```
var http = require("http"); http.
createServer(function(request, response) { response.
writeHead(200, {"Content-Type": "text/plain"});
request.on("data", function(chunk) { response.
write(chunk.toString().toUpperCase()); }); request.
on("end", function() { response.end(); });
}).listen(8000);
```

The chunk variable passed to the data handler will be a binary Buffer that can be transformed to a string by calling its toString method, which decodes it from the default encoding (UTF-8).

The following code, being run simultaneously with the server, will send a request to the server and output the received response:

```
var http = require("http");
var request = http.request({
  hostname: "localhost",
  port: 8000,
  method: "POST"
}, function(response) {
  response.on("data", function(chunk) {
    process.stdout.write(chunk.toString());
  });
});
request.end("Hello server");
```

The example writes to *process.stdout* (the standard output of the process, which is a writable stream), and not to *console.log*. We can't use *console. log*, since it adds an extra line feed after each piece of code—this is not necessary here.

Simple File Server

Let's combine our new knowledge about HTTP servers and working with the file system, and build a bridge between them: An HTTP server that provides remote access to files. Such a server has many use cases. It enables web applications to store and share data, or it can give a group of people access to a set of files.

When we consider files as resources over the HTTP protocol, the make, put, and delete methods can be used to read, write, and delete files. We will interpret the path in the request as the path to the file.

We do not need to open access to the entire file system, so we will interpret these paths as set relative to the root directory, and this will be the directory where the script runs. If I run the server from /home/marein/public/ (or C:\ Users\marijn\public\on Windows), while the request for /file.txt must point to/home/marijn/public/file.txt (or C:\Users\marijn\public\file.txt).

We will develop the program gradually, using the methods object to store functions that handle different HTTP methods.

```
var http = require("http"), fs = require("fs");

var methods = Object.create(null);

http.createServer(function(request, response) {
  function respond(code, body, type) {
    if (!type) type = "text/plain";
    response.writeHead(code, {"Content-Type": type});
    if (body && body.pipe)
      body.pipe(response);
    else
      response.end(body);
  }
  if (request.method in methods)
    methods[request.method](urlToPath(request.url),
                            respond, request);
  else
    respond(405, "Method " + request.method +
            " not allowed.");
}).listen(8000);
```

This code will launch the server returning 405 errors. This code is used to indicate that the requested method is not supported by the server.

The response function is passed to functions that process various methods, and works as a callback to end the request. It accepts the HTTP status code, the body, and possibly the content type. If the passed body is a read-only stream, it will have a pipe method that is used to pass the read stream to the write stream. If not, it is assumed that it is either null (the body is empty), or a string, and then it is passed directly to the end response method.

To get the path from the URL in the request, the urlToPath function, using the built-in Node "url" module, parses the URL. It takes a path name, something like */file.txt*, decodes to remove the escape codes %20, and inserts a dot at the beginning to get the path relative to the current directory.

```
function urlToPath(url) {
 var path = require("url").parse(url).pathname;
 return "." + decodeURIComponent(path);
}
```

Do you think the urlToPath function is unsafe? You're right. Let's return to this question in the exercises.

We will arrange the GET method so that it returns a list of files when reading the directory, and the contents of the file when reading the file.

The question to fill in is what type of Content-Type header we should return when reading the file. Since the file can have anything, the server can't just return the same type for everyone. But NPM can help with this. The mime module (file content type indicators like text/plain are also called MIME types) knows the correct type for a huge number of file extensions.

By running the following npm command in the directory where the server script lives, you can use require ("mime") to query the type library.

```
npm install mime
npm http GET https://registry.npmjs.org/mime
npm http 304 https://registry.npmjs.org/mime
mime@1.2.11 node_modules/mime
```

When the requested file does not exist, the correct error code for this case is 404. We will use *fs.stat* to return information on the file to find out if there is such a file, and if it is not a directory.

```
methods.GET = function(path, respond) {
  fs.stat(path, function(error, stats) {
    if (error && error.code == "ENOENT")
      respond(404, "File not found");
    else if (error)
      respond(500, error.toString());
    else if (stats.isDirectory())
      fs.readdir(path, function(error, files) {
        if (error)
          respond(500, error.toString());
        else
          respond(200, files.join("\n"));
      });
    else
      respond(200, fs.createReadStream(path),
        require("mime").lookup(path));
  });
};
```

Since disk requests take time, *fs.stat* works asynchronously. When the file does not exist, *fs.stat* will pass an error object with the value "ENOENT" of the code property to the callback function. It would be great if Node defined different error types for different errors, but there is no such thing. Instead, it outputs confusing Unix-style codes.

We will issue all unexpected errors with the code 500, which indicates that there is a problem on the server—as opposed to codes starting with 4, which indicate a problem with the request. In some situations, this will not be quite accurate, but for a small sample program, this will be enough.

The stats object returned by *fs.stat* tells us everything about the file. For example, size—file size, mtime-modification date. Here we need to find out whether it is a directory or a regular file—the isDirectory method will tell us this.

To read the list of files in the directory, we use *fs.readdir*, and after another callback, we return it to the user. For regular files, we create a readable stream via *fs.createReadStream* and pass it in response, along with the content type that the "mime" module has issued for this file.

The DELETE processing code will be easier:

```
methods.DELETE = function(path, respond) {
  fs.stat(path, function(error, stats) {
```

```
  if (error && error.code == "ENOENT")
    respond(204);
  else if (error)
    respond(500, error.toString());
  else if (stats.isDirectory())
    fs.rmdir(path, respondErrorOrNothing(respond));
  else
    fs.unlink(path, respondErrorOrNothing(respond));
  });
};
```

You may be wondering why an attempt to delete a non-existent file returns the status 204 instead of an error. You can say that when you try to delete a non-existent file, since the file is no longer there, the request is already executed. The HTTP standard encourages people to make idempotent requests—that is, those in which repeated repetitions of the same action do not lead to different results.

```
function respondErrorOrNothing(respond) {
  return function(error) {
    if (error)
      respond(500, error.toString());
    else
      respond(204);
  };
}
```

When the HTTP response contains no data, you can use the status code 204 ("no content"). Since we need to provide callback functions that either report an error or return a 204 response in different situations, I wrote a special *respondErrorOrNothing* function that creates such a callback.

This is the PUT request handler:

```
methods.PUT = function(path, respond, request) {
  var outStream = fs.createWriteStream(path);
  outStream.on("error", function(error) {
    respond(500, error.toString());
  });
  outStream.on("finish", function() {
```

```
  respond(200);
});
request.pipe(outStream);
};
```

Here we do not need to check the existence of the file—if it exists, we will simply overwrite it. Again, we use pipe to transfer data from a read stream to a write stream, in our case, from a request to a file. If the thread cannot be created, an "error" event is created, which we report in the response. When the data is passed successfully, pipe will close both threads, which will trigger the "finish" event. And after that, we can report success with the code 204.

The full server script is available on the website: eloquentjavascript.net/code/file_server.js. You can download it and run it through Node to run your own file server. Of course, it can be changed and supplemented to solve exercises or experiments.

The curl command-line utility, which is publicly available on unix systems, can be used to create HTTP requests. The following fragment tests our server. The –X option is used to specify the request method, and –d is used to include the request body.

curl http://localhost:8000/file.txt

File not found

curl -X PUT -d hello http://localhost:8000/file.txt

curl http://localhost:8000/file.txt

hello

curl -X DELETE http://localhost:8000/file.txt

curl http://localhost:8000/file.txt

File not found

First request to file.txt fails because there is no file yet. The PUT request creates a file, and look—the next request successfully receives it. After deleting it via DELETE, the file is again missing.

Error Handling

There are six places in the file server code where we redirect exceptions when we don't know how to handle errors. Since exceptions are not passed automatically to callback functions, but are passed to them as arguments, they must be handled individually each time. This negates the advantage of exception handling, namely, the ability to centrally handle errors.

What happens when something actually throws an exception in the system? We don't use try blocks, so it will be passed to the very top of the call stack. In Node, this causes the program to stop executing and outputs the exception information (along with stack tracking) to standard output.

Therefore, our server will crash when there are problems in the code—as opposed to problems with asynchrony, which will be passed as arguments in the call function. If we need to handle all the exceptions that occur when processing the request, so that we accurately send the response, we need to add try/catch blocks in each callback.

This is not good. Many Node programs are written to use as little exception handling as possible, meaning that if an exception occurs, the program can't handle it, and so you have to crash.

Another approach is to use promises. They catch exceptions thrown by callback functions and pass them as errors. In Node, you can load the promise library and use it to handle asynchronous calls. Few Node libraries integrate promises, but they are usually quite simple to wrap. The excellent "promise" module with NPM contains a denodeify function that takes an asynchronous function like *fs.ReadFile* and converts it to a function that returns a promise.

WHAT IS SERVER-SIDE PROGRAMMING?

Server-side website programming basically involves selecting the content that is returned to the browser in response to requests. Server-side code handles tasks such as verifying sent data and requests, using databases to store and retrieve data, and sending the correct data to the client as needed.

Most large websites use server-side programming to dynamically display various data when needed, mostly taken from a database located on the server and sent to the client for display through some code.

Perhaps the most significant benefit of server-side programming is that it allows you to shape the content of a website for a specific user.

Server-side programming is very valuable because it allows you to effectively deliver information compiled for individual users and thus create a much better user experience.

Companies like Amazon use back-end programming to build research results for products, generate a targeted offer based on customer preferences and previous purchases, simplify orders, and so on. Banks use back-end programming to store accounting information and allow only authorized users to view and complete transactions. Instagram Facebook, Twitter, Instagram, and Wikipedia use the backend to highlight, distribute, and control access to interesting content.

The Node platform uses a V8 virtual machine that uses Google Chrome for server programming. Thanks to V8, the performance of Node rises up, as the intermediate stages of creating executable code are eliminated. Instead of generating bytecode or using an interpreter, it is compiled directly into native machine code. Due to the fact that Node applies JavaScript on the server side, there are the following advantages:

- Developers can create web applications in a single language, so that reduces the need for context switching when developing servers and clients. This ensures that code is shared between the client and the server, such as the code for verifying data entered in a form, or the code for game logic.

- The most popular JSON data exchange format is a proprietary format JavaScript.

- JavaScript is used in various NoSQL databases (for example, in CouchDB and MongoDB), so the connection to such databases is carried out in a natural form. For example, the wrapper and query language for the MongoDB database is JavaScript. The projection/information for the CouchDB database is also JavaScript.

- The purpose of compiling in Node.js is JavaScript, in addition to being currently there are a number of other programming languages compiled in JavaScript 4.

- Node uses a single virtual machine (V8) that is compatible with the ECMAScript 5 standard. In other words, you don't have to wait until all the new JavaScript tools associated with the Node platform are available in all browsers.

V8 AND OTHER ENGINES

V8 is the name of the JavaScript engine used in the Google Chrome and Chromium family of browsers. It is responsible for executing the JavaScript code that gets into the browser when working on the Internet. V8 provides a runtime environment for JavaScript. The DOM and other web platform APIs are provided by the browser.

The JS engine is independent of the browser it runs in. It was this fact that made possible the emergence and development of the platform Node. js. V8 was chosen as the engine for Node.js in 2009. As a result of the explosive growth in the popularity of Node.js V8 turned out to be an engine that in our days it is responsible for executing a huge amount of server-side JS code. The Node.js ecosystem is huge. Thanks to this, V8 is also used, through projects like Electron, in the development of desktop applications. It should be noted that, in addition to V8, there are other engines:

- The Firefox browser uses the SpiderMonkey engine.

- Safari uses JavaScriptCore (also called Nitro).

- Edge uses the Chakra engine.

These engines implement the ECMA-262 specification, also called ECMAScript.

The V8 engine is written in C++, and it is constantly being improved. It can run on many systems, particularly Mac, Windows, and Linux. V8 is constantly evolving, and the same can be said for other engines. This leads, in particular, to an increase in the performance of web browsers and the platform Node.js. Browser engine manufacturers are constantly competing for the speed of code execution, and this has been going on for many years. All this benefits users and programmers alike.

DIFFERENCES BETWEEN THE NODE.JS AND BROWSER

What is the difference between JS development for Node.js and browser programming? The similarity between these environments is that both use the same language. But the development of applications designed to run in the browser is very different from the development of server applications. Despite the use of the same language, there are some key differences that make these two types of development into completely different activities.

It should be noted that if someone who was previously engaged in frontend, begins to learn Node.js, he/she has a very serious opportunity to quickly master everything that is needed due to the fact that it will write in a language that is already familiar to that person. If the need to learn a new environment is added to the need to learn a new language, the task becomes much more complicated.

So the main difference between a client and a server is in the environment for which you have to program, in the ecosystems of these environments. In the browser, the main amount of work falls on performing various operations with web documents via the DOM, as well as the use of other web platform APIs, such as, mechanisms for working with cookies. All this in Node.js, of course not. There is no document object, no window object, and no other objects provided by the browser.

The browser, in turn, does not have the same programming mechanisms that are available in the Node.js environment and exist as modules that can be connected to the application. For example, this is an API for accessing the file system.

Another difference between client-side and server-side development in JS is that when working in the Node environment. The JS developer has full control over the environment. Unless you are developing an open source application that can be run anywhere, you know exactly, for example, on which version of Node.js will run your project. This is very convenient in comparison with the client environment, where your code has to work in the user's existing browser. In addition, it means that you can use the latest features of the language without fear of problems.

Since JavaScript is developing extremely fast, browsers simply do not have enough time quickly enough implement all its innovations. In addition, not all users work on the latest versions of browsers. As a result, developers who want to use something new in their programs have to take this into account, take care of the compatibility of their applications with the browsers used, which may result in the need to abandon modern JavaScript features. You can, of course, use the Babel transpiler to convert the code to a format compatible with the ECMAScript 5 standard, which is supported by all browsers, but when working with Node.js you won't need it.

Another difference between Node.js and browsers is that in Node.js uses the CommonJS module system, while browsers can observe the beginning of the implementation of the ES standard Modules. In practice, this means that it is currently in Node.js, for connecting external code, the require () construction is used, and in the browser code—import.

HOSTING FOR NODE.JS APPLICATIONS

The choice of hosting for Node.js applications depend on your needs. Here is a small list of hosting options that you can explore once you decide to deploy your app and make it public. First, we will consider simple options that have limited capabilities, and then—more complex, but also have more serious capabilities.

The Simplest Hosting Option: Local Tunnel

Even if your computer is assigned a dynamic IP address or you are behind an NAT, you can deploy your application on it and serve user requests to it using a local tunnel. This option is suitable for quickly organizing testing, for organizing a product demonstration, or for giving access to the application to a very small group of people. For organizing local tunnels, there is a very good service, ngrok, available for many platforms. Using ngrok, it is enough to execute a command like ngrok PORT and the port you specified will be available from the Internet. At the same time, if you use the free version of the service, you will have an address in the domain ngrok.io. If you decide to sign up for a paid subscription, you can use your own domain names, and, in addition, you can improve the security of the solution (using ngrok, you open access to your computer to the entire Internet).

Environments for Node.js Projects Deployment That Do Not Require Configuration

Glitch

Glitch is an interactive environment and platform for rapid application development that allows you to deploy them in subdomains glitch.com. This platform does not support its own user domains yet, and there are some limitations when working with it, but it is great for working on application prototypes. The Glitch design looks pretty funny (perhaps this can be written in the advantages of this platform), but this is not some "toy," extremely limited environment. Here you can work with Node.js, Content Delivery Network (CDN), secure storage for sensitive information, data sharing with GitHub, and more. The Glitch project is handled by the same company that is behind FogBugz and Trello (it is also one of the creators of StackOverflow). I often use this platform to demonstrate applications.

Codepen

Codepen is a great platform around which an interesting community has formed. Here you can create projects that include multiple files and deploy them using your own domain.

Serverless Environments

Serverless platforms allow you to publish applications without having to think about servers, configuring them, or managing them at all. The serverless computing paradigm is that applications publish as functions that respond to accesses to a network endpoint. This approach to application deployment is also called Functions As A Service (FAAS).

Google Cloud Platform

Google Cloud is a great environment for Node deployment.js applications. Here is the relevant section of its documentation.

VPS hosting

There are many platforms that provide VPS hosting services. A common feature of such platforms is the fact that the developer gets a virtual server at his disposal, independently installs an operating system (Linux or Windows) on it, and independently deploys applications. Among the platforms that provide VPS services, of which there are a great many, you can note the following that I have used and that I could recommend to others:

- Digital Ocean

- Linode

- Amazon Web Services

PaaS Solutions

PaaS (Platform as a Service) are platforms that take care of many things that, under normal circumstances, the developer deploying the application should take care of.

Zeit Now

Zeit is an interesting option for deploying applications. Deployment, when using this platform, is reduced to entering the now command in the terminal. There is a free version of Zeit, provided that there are some restrictions when working with it. There is also a paid, more powerful version of this platform. Using Zeit, you can simply not think about the fact that your application needs a server to work. You simply deploy the application, and everything else is the responsibility of this platform.

Nanobox

The creators of the Nanobox platform, which includes the deployment of Node.js applications, call it PAAS V2.

Heroku

Heroku is another great platform for hosting Node.js applications.

Microsoft Azure

Azure is a cloud platform from Microsoft. Its documentation has a section dedicated to Node.js applications.

Standard Server

Another hosting solution is to buy (or rent, for example, using the Vultr Bare Metal service) a standard server, install Linux and other software on it, connect it to the Internet, and host Node.js applications on it. Hosting is a huge topic, but we hope that the materials in this section will allow you to choose exactly what you need.

NODE.JS FRAMEWORKS

Most probably, a beginner with Node.js will not want to reinvent the wheel when it comes to parsing a POST request, routing a URL, or forming a view. In these cases, you will most likely want to use one of the popular web frameworks. This section provides an overview of the main ones.

The Main Advantages of the Node.js Frameworks

Features such as better performance, functionality, high speed, and scalability make the Node.js are the number one choice for enterprise-level application development for large companies.

With Node.js can use the same language for both the frontend and backend. This will save you from the need to learn and apply new YAP.

Following are some of the main advantages:

- High-speed functions

- Support for data streaming

- Real-time operation

- Have solutions for all database queries

- Easy to write code

- Open-source code

- Cross-platform

- Working with a proxy server

- High performance

- Solving synchronization problems

- Friendly community

Express.js

At the moment, Express is the most suitable framework for most Node. js developers. It is relatively mature and built on the base of connect. Supports features such as routing, configuration, template engine, POST request parsing, and more.

While Express is already quite a solid framework, it is used on a much smaller scale compared to such analogues as Rails, CakePHP, or Django. Express is more comparable to a tool like Sinatra and, unfortunately, has not yet made much effort to move away from the Ruby roots toward something more natural for JavaScript. Anyway, using it is much easier and faster than creating your own framework, and at the moment it is the most worthy choice.

Express   🔍 search   **Home**   Getting started   Guide   API reference   Advanced topics   Resources

Express 4.17.1
Fast, unopinionated, minimalist web framework for Node.js

```
$ npm install express --save
```

🔥 Express 5.0 alpha documentation is now available.
The alpha API documentation is a work in progress. For information on what's in the release, see the Express release history.

Express.js includes the attached properties, such as simplified multiple routing, database integration, template engines, and so on. Moreover, advanced Node.js developers can also write extensions, plugins, and packages for it. Well-known websites and applications, such as Geekli.st, MySpace, Yummly, Klout, and Segment.io built on Express.js.

Express gives you the flexibility to use any signature-matching template engine, any user authentication scheme, and any third-party database. It will help you determine the structure of the project directory in a way that is convenient for you.

Express.js is a Node.js web application server platform specifically designed for creating single-page, multi-page, and hybrid web applications. This has become the standard server platform for Node.js. Express is the inner part of what is known as the MEAN stack.

MEAN is a free, open-source JavaScript software stack for creating dynamic websites and web applications that has the following components:

- Mongodb-Standard NoSQL Database

- Express.js is the default web application platform.

- Angular.js-JavaScript MVC framework used for web applications.

- Node.js is a platform used for scalable server and network applications.

Express.js environment makes it very easy to develop an application that can be used to handle multiple types of requests, such as GET, PUT, POST, and DELETE requests.

Installing and Using Express

Express is installed via the NPM. You can do this by running the following line on the command line:

```
npm install express
```

The above command asks the NPM to download the necessary express modules and install them accordingly.

Let's use our newly installed Express platform and create a simple "Hello World" app.

Our application is going to create a simple server module that will listen for the port number 3000. In our example, if a request is made through the browser to this port number, the server application will send a "Hello" World "response to the client.

```
var express=require('express');
var app=express();
app.get('/',function(req,res)
{
res.send('Hello World!');
});
var server=app.listen(3000,function() {});
```

In our first line of code, we use the require function to enable the "express module". Before we can start using the express module, we need to make an object out of it. Here we create a callback function. This function will be called whenever someone views the root of our web application, which is http://localhost: 3000. The callback function will be used to send the string "Hello World" to the web page. In the callback function, we send the string "Hello World" back to the client. The res parameter is used to send the content back to the web page. This "res" parameter is what is provided by the "request" module to allow content to be sent back to the web page. We then use the listening function to have our server application listen for client requests on port #3000. Here you can specify any available port.

If the command is successful, when running the code in the browser, going to the localhost URL on port 3000, you will see the string "Hello World" displayed on the page.

Routing
Routing defines the way an application responds to a client request to a specific endpoint.

For example, a client can make an http GET, POST, PUT, or DELETE request for various URLs, such as the ones shown below:

http://localhost:3000/Books
http://localhost:3000/Teachers

In the example above, If a GET request is made for the first URL, then ideally the response should be a list of books. If a GET request is made for the second URL, then ideally the response should be a list of teachers. Thus, based on the URL that is being accessed, other functions will be called on the web server, and, accordingly, the response will be sent to the client. This is the concept of routing. Each route can have one or more handler functions that are executed when the route is mapped.

Hapi.js

Hapi.js is the best Node.js web framework, which is used for developing application program interfaces. Thanks to a strong plugin system Hapi.js, you can fully manage the development process. Hapi motivates the developer to focus on the re-use logic instead of spending time building the infrastructure.

API   Tutorials   Resources   Policies   Modules   Plugins   Shop   Support

The Simple, Secure Framework
Developers Trust

Build **powerful**, **scalable applications**, with **minimal overhead** and full **out-of-the-box** functionality - your code, your way

Get started with hapi

It is mainly known for its robust plugin system and numerous key features consisting of configuration-based functionality, input validation, error handling, caching implementation, and logging. This framework is especially useful for passing a database connection.

Its simple design makes it easy to get started. At its core, Hapi uses many of the latest features of ES6 JavaScript, such as ES6 promises. For those of you who have used Express before, Hapi lets you try something new and experience all the latest JavaScript features. This framework is used by such large companies as Concrete, PayPal, Disney, and Wal-Mart.

Features of Hapi.js

- Powerful input data validation

- Functionality

- Caching implementation
- Improved error handling system

Let's move on to the installation of Hapi.js. We will use NPM to download Hapi.js, as well as its dependencies for our project. To do this, in the project directory, do the following:

```
npm install hapi.js
```

This downloads Hapi.js from NPM and installs it in our project directory. At the same time, any dependencies that can be relied on Hapi.js, are also uploaded for our convenience.

Koa.js

Koa.js—this is a minimal and flexible Node.js web application infrastructure, which provides a robust set of features for web and mobile applications. It is an open source framework developed and maintained by the creators of Express.js, the most popular web framework for nodes.

The purpose of the development was to fill in the shortcomings of Express.js. Due to the uniqueness of the script and methods, Koa can work in different browsers. It also works without using callbacks and has a powerful error handling system.

Features of Koa.js:

- Using the necessary generators to manage and process callbacks
- Effective error handling procedures

- Component-based blocks

- Cascading middleware model and no callback hell

Koa has a small footprint (600 lok) and is a very thin layer of abstraction above the Node for creating server-side applications. It is fully pluggable and has a huge community. It also allows us to easily extend Koa and use it according to our needs. It is built using advanced technology (ES6), which gives it an advantage over older platforms like Express.

To start developing using the Koa infrastructure, you need to install Node and npm. Make sure that the node and npm are installed by running the following commands in your terminal.

```
$node --version
$npm --version
```

Make sure that your node version is higher than 6.5.0. Now that we have Node and npm configured, let's figure out what npm is and how to use it.

Once we've set up development, it's time to start developing our first application using Koa. Create a new file named app.js and enter the following into it:

```
var koa = require('koa');
var app = new koa();
app.use(function* (){
    this.body = 'Hello world!';
});

app.listen(3000, function(){
    console.log('Server running on https://
localhost:3000')
});
```

Save the file, go to your terminal, and enter.

```
$ nodemon app.js
```

This will start the server. To test this app, open a browser and go to https://localhost: 3000 and you should get the "Hello World!" message.

How does this app work? The first line imports the Koa into our file. We have access to its API via the Koa variable. We use it to create an app and assign it to the var app.

- **app.use (function):** this function is a middleware that is called whenever our server receives a request. We'll learn more about middleware in the following chapters. The callback function is a generator, which we will see in the next chapter. The context of this generator is called the context in Koa. This context is used to access and modify the request and response objects. We set the body of this response as Hello world!

- **app.listen (port, function):** this function binds and listens for connections on the specified port. Port is the only required parameter here. The callback function is executed if the application is running successfully.

Routing

Web frameworks provide resources such as HTML pages, scripts, images, etc. along different routes. Koa does not support routes in the main module. We need to use the Koa-router module to easily create routes in Koa. Install this module using the following command.

```
npm install --save koa-router
```

Now that we have a Koa router installed, let's look at a simple example of a GET route.

```
var koa = require('koa');
var router = require('koa-router');
var app = koa();

var _ = router();                //Instantiate the
router
_.get('/hello', getMessage);     // Define routes

function *getMessage() {
   this.body = "Hello world!";
};
```

```
app.use(_.routes());        //Use the routes
defined using the router
app.listen(3000);
```

If we launch our app and go to localhost: 3000/hello, the server will receive a get request along the route "/hello". Our Koa app performs a callback function attached to this route and sends "Hello World!" as a response.

Total.js

Total.js was created by Peter Shirka, a programmer from Slovakia, in 2013. Then in 2013, Node.js was just gaining popularity. The main idea of the developer was to create a kernel that would have a large basic functionality, while not having to install a large number of additional dependencies, unlike Express.js, which has a small amount of basic functionality, and you need to expand it at the expense of external modules. Total.js can also be extended with different modules from npm. Art architecture Total.js something reminds me of Rails for Ruby or the Laravel framework for PHP.

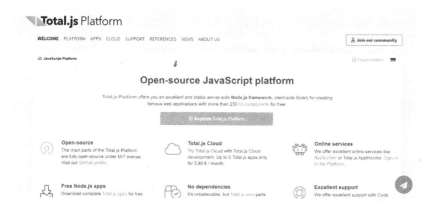

Total.js requires minimal maintenance and provides high performance and flawless scaling. Team Total.js It tries to meet the requirements of users in order to make the platform convenient and attractive for users around the world. For this reason, the Total.js has every chance to gain popularity in the coming years.

Features of Total.js:

- Software architecture according to the scheme: model-view-controller

- Extensible and asynchronous framework

- Provides full support for the RESTful routing engine

- Full support for websocket and media streaming protocols

Routing
Total.js supports classic routes, dynamic routes, and routes using regular expressions. You can write your own routes for dynamic content, files, or WebSocket.

Routes are declared in controllers, and each route defines a handler for the desired action. Routes also support flags. You can use flags to define special behavior, such as HTTP method, CORS, schema, intermediate processing, and so on.

Template Engine
The built-in template engine supports many functions and has excellent performance.

- Layouts

- Conditions, loops, and helpers

- Nested views

- Sections

Total.js it has become a whole platform, and it is also free, and now using these tools to launch your application will become even easier and faster. All open source projects that you can use in your eco-system:

1. **SuperAdmin:** The Node.js applications management system:

- Creating SSL certificates with

- SMS and email updates

- Personal access IDs for the API

- Easy integration with GIT

- Automatic backup via FTP

2. **Node.js CMS:** A simple, beautiful and design-oriented Total.js content management system with a lot of impressive features. Total.js CMS will help you easily manage your new interesting commercial or personal sites. Node.js CMS is built on a built-in NoSQL database and has no dependencies.

3. **OpenPlatform:** Enterprise container for third-party applications. OpenPlatform is a simple platform for running, integrating, and managing multiple third-party web applications. Provides running applications with a set of services, such as user management and security, so programmers can simply focus on the business logic. For example, on the basis of this solution, you can develop your own corporate CRM.

4. **Node.js Messenger:** A free alternative to Slack with similar functionality. A small, fast, open-source web application that you can customize to suit your needs.

5. **Flow:** Visual programming interface for real-time data processing. Designed for the Internet of Things, as well as classic web/REST applications and much more. You can also add it to any existing application Total.js (framework + 2.5. x).

6. **Node.js Eshop:** A small business e-commerce solution written in Node.js. A full-fledged store built on the platform of another tool from Total.js CMS. From the cms, there are also sets of widgets, post editors. As in any full-fledged store, there is a functionality for searching and editing products and orders, plus paypal for payment.

7. **Node.js Helpdesk:** The solution will help you solve your customers' problems much faster. Register your customers in the system and allocate them prepaid monthly minutes. Their problems can be easily solved by your support team.

8. **Node.js Wiki:** A simple tool/application for creating documentation in Wiki form. Documents are created using the Markdown format.

Derby.js

An MVC framework that makes it easier to write real-time collaboration applications that work as in Node.js, and in browsers. Just a couple of days ago, the main branch was changed in the Derby repository.

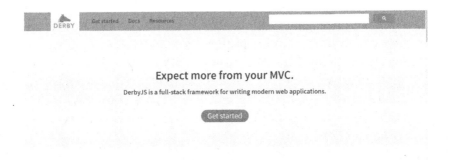

It provides seamless data synchronization between the server and the client. Derby.js is well known as the full-stack Node framework.js for writing modern web applications. You can use it to create custom code and develop high-performance web applications. Thanks to its unique characteristics, the Derby.js is gaining popularity nowadays.

Features of the Derby.js:

- MVC template for both client and server side

- Ideal for mobile and web application development

- Using server-side rendering for fast page loading, HTML templates, and search engine support

Mojito.js

Mojito is a JavaScript web framework that allows you to write programs for the client and server side. For server-side Node.js is used. With Mojito, developers will no longer have to write different backend and frontend code. If JavaScript is not enabled in the browser, the Mojito application will still be executed on the server side, using the same code. The framework is based on the well-known JavaScript library Yahoo!—YUI 3 (Yahoo! User Interface Library).

Mojito is another powerful mobile app development platform created by the Yahoo Developer Network. Mojito also acts as an MVC application framework and can build high-performance mobile and web applications using JavaScript, CSS3, and HTML5.

Mojito offers the development of high-performance and standard cross-platform applications that run on both the client and server side, since the client and server components are written in JavaScript. It also provides a convenient way to collect data and is ideal for on-premises development environments and tools.

It works as a module that connects very well to other core Node modules. Mojito is suitable for simplifying the localization and internationalization of libraries.

The Mojito framework is available on GitHub and is distributed under the BSD license.

Adonis.js

AdonisJs is one of the most popular Node.js frameworks running on all major operating systems. It has a static ecosystem for writing server-side web applications. Thus, you can choose the appropriate package, focusing on specific business needs.

Adonis is a real MVC framework for Node.js with the right framework. It carries the concepts of service providers from the popular Laravel PHP framework for creating large-scale applications, as well as using all the features of ES6 to make your code more accurate and supported.

The infrastructure supports convenient authentication, SQL ORM (relational object maps), migration, and database replenishment. The AdonisJs architecture is similar to the Laravel web infrastructure architecture for PHP applications and has the same folder structure and several similar configuration concepts.

By default, AdonisJs uses the Edge template system, designed for intuitive use. Like Laravel, AdonisJs has an ORM system called Lucid, which serves as an interface for interaction between the application models and the database. With AdonisJs, developers can create complex applications where the backend is responsible for applying business logic, routing, and rendering all the pages of the application. You can also create a web services API to return JSON responses from the controller. These web services can be used with client-side frameworks such as Vue.js, React, and Angular.

Features of Adonis.js

- Support for an ORM consisting of SQL databases

- Efficient creation of an active record-based SQL query

- Easy-to-learn query builder for creating simple and fast queries

- Providing support for No-SQL databases such as Mongodb

Installing the Adonis CLI

Let's install the Adonis CLI and all its required packages on our local computer. The CLI allows you to create the structure of a new AdonisJs project, as well as create and generate templates for controllers, binders, and models in your application. You will also create a database for the project.

Run the following command to globally install the AdonisJs CLI on a computer using npm:

```
npm i -g @adonisjs/cli
```

After the installation process is complete, enter the following command in the terminal to confirm the installation of AdonisJs and view the current version:

```
adonis -version
```

You will see the output indicating the current version of Adonis.js.

We have successfully installed the AdonisJS CLI and can now use the adonis command to install new AdonisJs projects, manage projects, and generate the required files, including controllers, models, etc.

Keystone.js

Keystone.js is a content management system and framework for creating server-side applications that interact with a database. It is based on the Express platform for Node.js and uses MongoDB for data storage. It is an alternative to CMS for web developers who want to create a data-driven website, but do not want to move to the PHP platform or to large systems such as WordPress.

While WordPress can be configured by non-very technical users, KeystoneJS offers the control that professional users need to develop new websites, although it is still significantly easier to work with KeystoneJS than to create a website manually from scratch. It not only offers a platform for building websites; you can replace almost everything on it and develop more specialized systems, such as apps and APIs.

KeystoneJS is built on the basis of Node.js/JavaScript platform, which makes it potentially more productive than WordPress, on top of PHP for specific applications. The strong point in favor of this platform is the availability of packages; if you need it, there's probably one that does what you want.

Database

KeystoneJS uses MongoDB to store all of its data. MongoDB is one of the most popular non-relational databases on the market, and it is often used by Node developers.js thanks to its ease of use in JavaScript projects.

Since KeystoneJS is more like a library rather than a ready-to-use system, almost everything can be customized if you know JavaScript. Because it is based on Node.js, Express, and Mongoose, you get almost the same freedom; you just have a few extra things to work with faster.

Template Engine

You can also choose between some template engines in WordPress (like Timber) that allow you to use a different language to write topics that are easier to read, similar to other template languages from different platforms.

Key Features

1. **Automatically generated admin user interface:** When you create something with Keystone.js, the data models you define are also used to automatically create an admin panel to manage your data. You don't need to install database models directly; you describe your data using lists.

2. **Lightweight and easy to set up:** The fact that you get control of everything without having to know the huge system inside out makes the sites easy and easy to set up.

3. **Easily extensible:** KeystoneJS can be considered a library, and you are not limited to using only the features it provides. You can easily integrate any package from one of the largest library ecosystems: JavaScript.

4. **Start from scratch or use a template:** If you want to start creating something like a blog, you don't need to spend time learning the logic of the system; KeystoneJS provides ready-made templates to use or customize. If you have specific requirements, you can start from scratch using the tools they provide, but without having to write everything yourself.

5. **Specially designed for developers:** Other CMSs tend to include everything in one package, so that non-technical users can get started as quickly as possible. However, KeystoneJS is aimed at developers who want to create a CMS, but don't want to inflate or limit the finished systems.

6. **Compatible with third-party services:** KeystoneJS offers integration with some useful third-party services such as Amazon S3, Cloudinary, Mandrill out of the box. Suppose you want to store certain data in Amazon S3, it's as simple as adding a {type: Types. S3File} field type when you define your data.

Use Cases

1. **Websites for non-technical users:** If you work as a web developer for clients, you may find that the task of creating a website for a non-technical person is not so easy, since you also need to create an administration panel to add and update. data. With KeystoneJS, you don't have to worry about doing double work; the admin panel is created automatically.

2. **Dynamic Websites:** KeystoneJS provides a useful framework and tools for working with dynamic data on websites, useful when static websites are too small to consider, but traditional CMSs like WordPress are too heavy or questionable for your project.

3. **Performance:** There is nothing better than creating something just for your needs; If you need a highly specialized website and performance is key, you can use KeystoneJS to create something that meets your needs and takes advantage of the performance of the Node platform.js, especially for parallel services.

4. **Ecosystem:** JavaScript has one of the richest ecosystems of third-party packages. Also, if you need (or just prefer) to use JavaScript on both the client and server, KeystoneJS is a great tool.

5. **Tight Deadline:** Do you have a project with specialized features, and the deadline is very close? The way KeystoneJS handles the data, and the fact that the admin panel is created automatically, means that you can spend more time creating the actual logic of your site instead of handling the implementation details.

Socket.IO

This is the best Node.js server and web framework for creating real-time web applications. It enables event-based communication between the Node.js server and the browser. Socket.IO acts as a backend library for Node.js and as a frontend library in the browser.

Main properties Socket.IO they consist of binary streaming, asynchronous I/O processing, and instant messaging. The framework allows for real-time concurrency for document collaboration needs.

Socket.IO is compatible with all operating systems, devices, and browsers. This framework is used by top technology companies, such as Microsoft, Trello, Yammer, and Zendesk.

Socket.IO is the solution around which most real-time systems are built, providing a bidirectional communication channel between the client and the server. This means that the server can send messages to clients. Whenever an event occurs, the idea is that the server will receive it and send it to interested connected clients.

Working with Socket.IO

To start development using Socket.IO, you need to install Node and npm. If you don't have them, go to the Node setup to install the Node on your local system. Make sure that the Node and npm are installed by running the following commands in your terminal.

```
node --version
npm --version
```

You should get an output showing the latest version of Node and npm that is installed on your system.

Open your terminal and type the following in your terminal to create a new folder, and enter the following commands:

```
$ mkdir test-project
$ cd test-proect
$ npm init
```

After answering the questions, you will have a configuration file "package.json node.js". Now you need to install Express and Socket.IO. To install them and save them in the package.json file, enter the following command on your terminal in the project directory.

```
npm install --save express socket.io
```

And the last thing is that we have to keep restarting the server. When we make changes, we will need a tool called nodemon. To install nodemon, open your terminal and type the following command:

```
npm install -g nodemon
```

Whenever you need to start the serve, instead of using the Node app.js use nodemon app.js. This ensures that you don't have to restart the server every time the file changes. This speeds up the development process.

```
Socket.IO - Namespaces
```

Socket.IO allows you to "name" your sockets, which essentially means assigning different endpoints or paths. This is a useful feature that allows you to minimize the number of resources (TCP connections) and at the same time separate the problems in your application by separating the communication channels. Multiple namespaces actually use the same WebSockets connection, which allows us to save socket ports on the server.

Namespaces are created on the server side. However, clients join them by sending a request to the server.

ActionHero.js

ActionHero is one of the most well-known API frameworks. It will help you quickly develop scalable and reusable Nodes.js API servers for your projects. ActionHero acts as a toolkit that will allow you to build such API servers that will initially work together with existing applications and platforms. With tens of thousands of users, you can always find the right answers and ideas to ensure a daily efficient workflow with ActionHero.

The goal of ActionHero is to create an easy-to-use set of tools for creating reusable and scalable APIs for HTTP, WebSockets, and others. It was built from the ground up to include all the features we expect from a modern API platform.

The type of workload that ActionHero does well includes creating and using APIs, storing and retrieving data from databases, modifying files, and similar tasks.

ActionHero has 5 key concepts that make up each application: actions, tasks, initializers, chat, and servers.

ActionHero can be installed via NPM, Yarn and many other ways. To install it via NPM, type the following commands:

```
npm install actionhero --save
npx actionhero generate
npm install
npm start
```

To install it via Yarn, type the following commands:

```
yarn add actionhero
yarn run actionhero generate
yarn add ws ioredis jest standard
yarn run actionhero
```

ASYNCHRONOUS PROGRAMMING

JavaScript itself is a synchronous, single-threaded programming language. This means that you can't create new threads running in parallel in your code. However, computers are inherently asynchronous. That is, certain actions can be performed independently of the main thread of the program execution. In modern computers, each program is allocated a certain amount of processor time, when this time expires, the system gives resources to another program, also for some time. Such switches are performed cyclically, it is done so quickly, that a person simply can't notice it, as a result, we think that our computers are running many programs at the same time. But this is an illusion (if we do not talk about multiprocessor machines).

In the bowels of programs, interrupts are used—signals that are transmitted to the processor and allow you to attract the attention of the system. We will not go into details, the most important thing is to remember that asynchronous behavior, when the execution of a program is suspended until the moment when it needs CPU resources, is completely normal. At a time when the program does not load the system with work, the computer can solve other tasks. For example, in this approach, when a program waits for a response to a network request it has made, it does not block the processor until it receives a response.

As a rule, programming languages are asynchronous, some of them give the programmer the opportunity to manage asynchronous mechanisms, using either the built-in language tools or specialized libraries. We are talking about such languages as C, Java, C#, PHP, Go, Ruby, Swift,

Python. Some of them allow you to program in an asynchronous style using threads, launching new processes.

Asynchrony in JavaScript

As already mentioned, JavaScript is a single-threaded synchronous language. Lines of code written in JS, they are executed in the order in which they are present in the text, one after the other. For example, here is a fairly common JS program that demonstrates this behavior:

```
const a = 3
  const b = 2
  const c = a * b
  console.log(c)
  doSomething()
```

But JavaScript was created for use in browsers. Its main task, at the very beginning, was to organize the processing of events related to user activity. For example, these are events such as onClick, onMouseOver, onChange, onSubmit, and so on. How to solve such problems in the framework of a synchronous programming model? The answer lies in the environment in which JavaScript runs.

Namely, the browser allows you to effectively solve such problems, giving the programmer the appropriate APIs. In the Node environment.js has tools for performing non-blocking I/O operations, such as working with files, organizing data exchange over the network, and so on.

Callbacks

If we talk about browser-based JavaScript, we can note that you cannot know in advance when the user clicks on a certain button. In order to ensure the system's response to such an event, a handler is created for it. The event handler accepts a function that will be called when the event occurs. It looks like this:

```
document.getElementById('button').addEventListener
('click', () = > {
//the user clicked on the element
})
```

Such functions are also called callback functions or callbacks. A callback is a normal function that is passed as a value to another function. It will only be called when an event occurs. JavaScript implements the concept of first-class functions. Such functions can be assigned to variables and passed to other functions (called higher-order functions). In client-side JavaScript development, a common approach is to wrap all client code in a window object's load event listener, which calls the callback passed to it after the page is ready to work:

```
window.addEventListener ('load', () = > {
//page loaded
/ / now you can work with it
})
```

Callbacks are used everywhere, not just for handling DOM events. For example, we have already met with their use in timers:

```
setTimeout(() => {
// performed in 2 seconds
}, 2000)
```

Error Handling in Callbacks

Let's talk about how to handle errors in callbacks. There is one common strategy for handling such errors, which is also used in Node.js. It consists in the fact that the first parameter of any callback function is an error object. If there are no errors, the null value will be written to this parameter. Otherwise, there will be an error object containing its description and additional information about it. Here's what it looks like:

```
fs.readFile('/file.json', (err, data) => {
if (err !== null) {
//handling the
console.log(err)
return error
}
//no errors, handling
the console. log (data)
})
```

What Is "Promises"?

Starting with the ES6 standard, new features are introduced in JavaScript that make it easier to write asynchronous code, allowing you to do without callbacks. We are talking about the promises that appeared in ES6, and about the async/await construct introduced in ES8.

Promises are one of the ways to work with asynchronous program constructs in JavaScript, which, in general, reduces the use of callbacks.

Promises are usually defined as proxy objects for certain values that are expected to appear in the future. Promises are also called "promises" or "promised results." Although this concept has been around for many years, promises were standardized and added to the language only in ES2015. ES2017 introduced the async/await construct, which is based on promises, and which can be considered as a convenient replacement for them. Therefore, even if you don't plan to use the usual promises, understanding how they work is important for effective use of the async/await construct.

After calling the promise, it goes into the pending state. This means that the function that called the promise continues to execute, while some calculations are performed in the promise, after which the promise reports this. If the operation performed by the promise completes successfully, the promise is transferred to the "fulfilled" state. Such a promise is said to be successfully resolved. If the operation fails, the promise is moved to the "rejected" state.

What Is Async/Await Construction?

The async/await design represents a modern approach to asynchronous programming, simplifying it. Asynchronous functions can be represented as a combination of promises and generators, and, in general, this construction is an abstraction over promises.

The async/await design allows you to reduce the amount of template code that you have to write when working with promises. When promises appeared in the ES2015 standard, they were aimed at solving the problem of creating asynchronous code. They coped with this task, but in the two years that separated the release of the ES2015 and ES2017 standards, it became clear that they could not be considered the final solution to the problem.

One of the problems that promise solved was the famous "hell of callbacks", but they solved this problem and created their own problems of a similar nature.

Promises were simple constructs around which something with a simpler syntax could be constructed. As a result, when the time came, the async/await construct appeared. Its use allows you to write code that looks like synchronous, but is asynchronous, in particular, does not block the main thread.

Generating Events in Node.js

If you've worked with JavaScript in the browser, you know that events play a huge role in processing user interactions with pages. We are talking about processing events caused by mouse clicks and movements, keystrokes on the keyboard, and so on. In Node.js can work with events that the programmer creates independently. Here you can create your own event system using the events module. In particular, this module offers us the EventEmitter class, the capabilities of which can be used to organize work with events. Before using this mechanism, you need to connect it:

```
const EventEmitter = require('events').EventEmitter
```

When working with it, we can use the *on()* and *emit()* methods, among others. The emit method is used to call events. The on method is used to configure callbacks, event handlers that are called when a specific event is called.

At this point, we have covered a good deal of ground as far as Node programming is concerned. We are now familiar with numerous common Node frameworks, Node modules as well as concepts such as Asynchronous programming and Server-Side scaling.

As such, we are now ready to get started with additional Node.js frameworks, and take a closer look at some of the most vital ones.

CHAPTER 4

Polymer

Now that we are done with the basics of Node.js, it is time to turn our attention toward something else. In this chapter, we will be focusing on Google Polymer, an innovative and very useful JavaScript (JS) library that has risen in popularity ever since it was born.

Essentially, Polymer is not a mainstream "framework" per se. Instead, it is a JS library. But much like a JS framework, Polymer too revolves primarily around data encapsulation and reusability, as we will soon see in the course of this chapter. This means Polymer can find great applications and usage among modern day web applications, especially when the goal is to save development time.

Polymer comes with a 3-Clause BSD license and is, naturally, fully open source. It is used by a wide range of Google services and applications, as well as by many others.

Before going any further, we must first understand what Polymer can accomplish and how it works. Following that, we will get started with installation, setup and usage.

INTRODUCTION TO POLYMER

Introducing Polymer is not a complicated task and even the most basic level JS coders can quickly grasp its underlying concepts. This is because unlike the bigger JS frameworks out there, Polymer focuses on a specific set of tasks and not a multitude of goals and tasks.

DOI: 10.1201/9781003203711-4

What Is Polymer?

As we mentioned above, if we are to follow the textbook definition, Polymer is a JS library and not a full-fledged JS framework. However, its modus operandi and purpose overlap heavily with those of JS frameworks and is, as such, often clubbed under JS frameworks.

Polymer is maintained and curated by Google, along with a loyal community of users.

Broadly speaking, Polymer is used to develop web applications using Web Components as the underlying tool. Now, what are these Web Components?

Here is how the Polymer GitHub page describes Web Components:[1]

Web components are an incredibly powerful new set of primitives baked into the web platform, and open up a whole new world of possibility when it comes to componentizing front-end code and easily creating powerful, immersive, app-like experiences on the web.

But that does not make it very clear, does it?

Let us put it this way. Web Components are reusable elements or blocks of elements that you can make use of in your web applications and projects. As such, you do not need to code everything from the ground up or scratch. You can import and reuse existing Web Components to do common tasks in your projects, and then further code additional functionality to suit your needs. This can, very clearly, save your development time and efforts and also ease the overall development process.

Now, isn't it clear why Polymer's functionality overlaps with those of JS frameworks? In spite of being a real JS library, Polymer can help you save time by not providing just blocks of code, but an entire range of "Components" around which you can build applications and projects. In other words, you can view Web Components, as provided by Polymer, as LEGO blocks or IKEA furniture, which comes in varied shapes, sizes, and variants but the primary purpose remains the same, helps you assemble and puts together things as per your requirements.

In fact, it is not uncommon for JS developers to use Polymer Web Components in assonance with Vue.js or React or even Angular. In fact, Polymer plays well with most other modern day JS libraries and

---

[1] See https://github.com/Polymer/polymer#overview

frameworks and its reusability of code can come very handy when building complex projects.

At this point, it might be a good idea to mention some of the major properties of Web Components:

Web Components in Polymer are symbolic or similar to HTML imports, pretty much like we are used to importing CSS stylesheets in themes or templates.

Just in case you are wondering, yes it is possible to code and build your own Web Components. As a matter of fact, custom Web Components are often reused and shared in the Polymer community by fellow developers.

It might also be worthwhile to learn about Shadow DOM in Polymer. As a JS developer, you might already be aware of the concept of DOM. Shadow DOM inserts a new node to your existing DOM; then it creates a boundary between your DOM and the new node.

How is Shadow DOM useful? Let us assume that we have a custom Web Component element that makes use of its own CSS styles. Now, what if we wish to reuse the same element in another project? There are chances that CSS styling can be overridden by that of the new project. To avoid this, the Shadow DOM is used to encapsulate portions or parts of our styling and scripting structure so that the element and Component's styles or scripts are not hampered by that of the new project.

You can find an assortment of Web Components over at https://www. webcomponents.org/ Many of these are related to Polymer, whereas many aren't. This shows that Web Components are not unique to Polymer, albeit it is a rather popular option for working with them in the world of JS.

Now that we have understood what Polymer is and how it tends to work by means of Web Components, it is time to learn more about its special features.

What Makes Polymer Special?

Perhaps the biggest selling point of Polymer is that it lets you create your own HTML elements that you can then use within your complex applications and projects. This means your apps are easier to maintain and fully scalable as you can modify Web Components and HTML elements to suit your requirements.

In other words, you do not need to rely heavily or entirely on scripts and markup. Instead, the focus shifts toward declarative usage of Web Components—simply declare the Components or elements that you wish to use (or reuse) in your projects, and you're done. With the level of abstraction and encapsulation that is provided in Polymer, it is ideal for mainstream everyday usage.

This is where Polymer becomes really different from other JS "libraries," say, jQuery. There is no custom requirement to focus on a given set of scripts or similar entities. Polymer believes in making use of native technology as offered by the web browser clients of today.

To better understand this concept, let us assume you have built an app in Polymer already. Now, how would you use this app if it were coded or built using some other JS library? You will probably be required to convert the app to make it suited for other libraries, or import a big range of dependencies. In Polymer though, your application is nothing more than an element. Thus, you can make use of it simply by importing it in any project of your choice, say an HTML page and adding a tag for it.

This is what makes Polymer special. No matter how complex your Polymer app is, at the end of the day, it is just another element that you import in your page. You can access their properties and methods with ease and even in other frameworks or libraries. More importantly, you can create entire complex applications using Polymer and even use them as just HTML elements.

Polymer is fully compatible with most other element libraries. Thus, pretty much like a JS framework, Polymer too does not pose compatibility issues and works seamlessly as per its structure and paradigm.

Major Pros and Cons of Polymer

Now that we have established what special features Polymer brings to the table, it is time to learn about some of its advantages and disadvantages.

Advantages

- As mentioned above, the biggest advantage of Polymer is that it saves development time and efforts by offering reusable Web Components for projects.

- Creating custom elements using Polymer is really easy and even the novice JS developers can master it in a short span of time.

- Polymer supports conditional templates as well as Shadow DOM, thereby providing better encapsulation and abstraction for your projects and easier control of the overall workflow.

- Polymer supports gesture events as well as computed properties. In fact, toward the end of this chapter when we discuss some of the major applications and existing projects that make use of Polymer, it will become evident that Polymer comes loaded with all the bells and whistles that you might need from a Web Component library.

- Polymer supports both one way and two way data binding models. However, it was recently (May 2018) announced that focus will eventually shift toward one way data binding and away from two way data binding.

Considering the fact that custom elements created using Polymer are reusable and compatible with other frameworks or development practices, adoption in existing projects is fairly straightforward. This is, by far, the biggest advantage of Polymer. It carries a universal appeal to itself owing to the notion of reusable Web Components.

Disadvantages
There is not much that can be spoken about Polymer's drawbacks. However, it does not come without its own share of caveats:

- This is not a disadvantage for most coders or users anymore. However, if your target audience is relying on primitive web browsers or out of date technology, Polymer may just render your project incompatible with the same. The real issue is that by implementing everything as an HTML element within a tag, Polymer removes the need for importing lots of scripts. However, this also means a lot of effort is put on the web browser. For modern web browsers, this is no issue at all and everything runs smooth. But for older web browsers, at times, such demands may be too much. This also applies to modern "lightweight" web browsers.

- The documentation and support tutorials have come a long way in recent years, but Polymer's docs are still nowhere near in comparison to those of, say, Vue.js or even Aurelia. In fact, Polymer's official documentation can really be confusing at times for some users.

- Polymer is nimble enough to not have any major performance issues. With that said, on some mobile platforms (albeit the lesser known ones, such as Tizen by Samsung), Web Components by Polymer take their own time to load. Even if everything works as planned, you still see some out of place whitespace on your web page or a blank page during load.

It is often argued that Polymer is something that works perfectly on a desktop web browser client but struggles on a mobile web browser client. This becomes more visible if you are relying on a mobile device with limited memory.

Rendering Polymer elements can cause a memory strain on mobile web browsers and if you are attempting to multi-task at the same time, frozen web pages can become common. Try using Google Earth or Allo for Web in a mobile web browser running on a device with low memory? Encountered some sluggish page performance? Exactly!

However, all of these negative aspects are more related to the device or client at hand and not directly to Polymer. After all, the majority of users nowadays do not rely on older web browsers and more and more devices now come with additional memory and better ability to run detailed HTML elements in web pages. However, if your target audience is from a minority with weaker hardware or software, be wary about using too many Polymer elements in your apps.

At this stage, we have completed our introduction to Polymer. We have learned what it is, what it can do and what are its major pros and cons. Now, we are ready to get started with Polymer and learn about its setup and installation and other related details.

HOW TO USE POLYMER?

In order to use Polymer for development, we first need to install it. We will now go through the installation steps in order to get Polymer ready for work.

Installing Polymer

Before going any further, our first step is to install Git. If you are already active in JS development, you must be having Git on your system as well. However, for folks who do not have Git set up, it is easy to download the relevant installer from https://git-scm.com/download/—there are installers available for Windows, Mac as well Linux platforms.

To verify your Git installation, you can issue a simple command to check the installed Git version, as follows:

```
git --version
```

If everything is installed properly, you will see the installed Git version therein.

The next step is to install Node.js and npm. Polymer will need the latest version of Node.js to work properly, so if you have an older version, it is a good idea to upgrade before going any further. If you are using the latest Node.js version or one with long term support, you can proceed further.

Node.js and npm too, just like Git, have their own set of installers available for various platforms, including Mac, Windows, and Linux. You can grab the relevant one from this page: https://nodejs.org/en/download/ Plus, if you are running Linux, it is advisable to compile Node.js from source, or install it using the command line. This will automatically ensure all dependencies are satisfied, the required repositories are added and the latest versions are installed right from the first day. Depending on your Linux distro, the command will vary. For Ubuntu and other Debian-family users, the following should work:

```
sudo apt install nodejs
```

The same steps should be repeated for npm. For Debian-family Linux users:

```
sudo apt install npm
```

Or, for Windows, Mac, and other platforms, running the required installation application. The Node.js documentation is rather diverse on this subject, and we will revisit this during the Node.js chapter.

Once you have successfully installed Node.js and npm, you can check your installation by verifying the versions, as follows:

```
npm --version
```

And also

```
node --version
```

If everything is in order, you will see the installed version details.

Now, we have the environment all set up. We have Git, npm, and Node.js on our system and can easily install Polymer Command Line Interface (CLI).

To download and install Polymer CLI, we will run the npm command as follows:

```
npm install -g polymer-cli
```

Depending on the number of dependencies that might need to be fetched, it can take some time to fully install Polymer CLI.

Once done, you might wish to confirm the status of Polymer installation. To do that, simply check for the version that is installed, as followed:

```
polymer --version
```

This should show you the Polymer version that is installed, assuming everything went right during the installation process. Otherwise, you may see an error.

As the name suggests, Polymer CLI is a command line interface for working with Polymer. It is a multipurpose tool that helps you build, serve and even test your Polymer projects. It has its own set of commands and is quite a helpful utility in its own right. You can find detailed documentation as well as relevant commands for Polymer CLI on https://www.polymer-project.org/3.0/docs/tools/polymer-cli

Serving a Polymer App

Now that you have Polymer installed and ready, it is time to learn how to structure and serve an app.

Note that we will be following the latest version of Polymer for this example. At the time of writing, it happens to be Polymer 3 (so Polymer 1.x or 2.x may not ascribe to the given format).

The first step will be to create a new folder for your app:

```
mkdir my-fancy-app
cd my-fancy-app
```

Thereafter, you can initialize your project with an app template:

```
polymer init
```

You can download the polymer-3-starter-kit at this point, so that Polymer CLI can initialize your app and set it up using the Polymer 3 Starter Kit template.

Following that, the commands to be followed are fairly straightforward. To serve your project:

```
polymer serve
```

The serve command, as is with many other JS projects, tells you where the application resides (in terms of IP addresses on the localhost). You can then browse it in the web browser and view your project live.

Of course, the above is just how to "get started" with a project. You will then need to add additional functionality and features and possibly integrate Polymer elements with bigger and more complex applications.

In terms of deployment of the app, you can sign up for one of the various services such as Google App Engine or Firebase, or even use your own custom cloud servers. The procedure varies from one case to another and is generally well-documented by the service you opt for, so you should check the required documentation.

Bear in mind though that in order to use Polymer apps or elements in external projects, you will need to have the project ready for integration. It is not uncommon, therefore, for web developers to build an application using Vue.js or React and then make use of Polymer elements therein.

But that does not imply that Polymer cannot be used to power a full-fledged web application. In fact, the Polymer team themselves have put together two proper web apps to serve as examples of what Polymer can be used to accomplish. You can check out the case studies for the Shop app at https://www.polymer-project.org/3.0/toolbox/case-study and the News app at https://www.polymer-project.org/3.0/toolbox/news-case-study

Building Progressive Web Apps Using Polymer

If you intend to build Progressive Web Apps using the Polymer library, you may find the Polymer App Toolbox useful.

This particular App Toolbox is a collection of resources, components, tools and templates that can be used to put together Progressive Web Apps in Polymer.

The Polymer App Toolbox follows the standardized practices based on Web Components and Polymer. It offers a fully responsive series of templates and supports localization as well as local storage for testing and debugging.

Detailed documentation related to the App Toolbox can be had at https://www.polymer-project.org/3.0/toolbox/In order to build Progressive Web Apps with the help of Polymer, using the Toolbox is quite possibly the easiest and fastest way.

CONCLUSION

In this chapter, we have familiarized ourselves with Polymer and its uses. We learned about its features, how it can prove useful, its advantages and disadvantages and also basic modes of operation with Polymer.

Now, before winding up this chapter, let us spend a moment learning about what Polymer is useful for in the real world.

The Polymer Ecosystem

Polymer is used by various services and products of Google, such as the new revamped look of YouTube. It is also employed by Google Play Music, Google Allo Messenger for Web and the redesigned version of Google Sites.

In essence, Polymer is useful when you wish to add elements that are to be reused on a regular basis. Therefore, for applications that revolve around a specific set of actions, such as a web-based interface for a community app, Polymer can provide you with custom HTML elements that can be reused as and when necessary.

Initially, reception for Polymer was rather on the lower side. This was because it was viewed as a library that was ahead of its time—certain browsers failed to handle Polymer components well and the only workaround was to bundle custom scripts, pretty much like jQuery. This, obviously, defeated the very purpose that Polymer stood for.

However, following the browser wars that saw the monumental rise of Chrome and Firefox and the absolute collapse of Internet Explorer, Polymer rose manifolds in popularity. Today, Polymer is gaining a lot of attention and its approach of import and reuse of Components is being appreciated by several developers.

If you are a JS developer looking to add some additional frameworks or libraries to your arsenal, Polymer is definitely something you should consider seriously. It is especially handy if you are primarily into building apps for the web and prefer to offer a near-native experience in web browsers.

Further Steps

Going forward, you can experiment more with Polymer and custom elements. It is a good idea to spend some time learning how to modify, customize and tweak elements so as to make them better apt and more suited for your needs.

Beyond that, you can also attempt building apps in Polymer, albeit more often than not, Polymer finds practical usage in element building that are to be imported in apps that are in turn managed by some larger framework. This, being frank, is the mainstream approach and you can choose to ignore it too.

Suggested Resources

To learn more about development with Polymer:

- **The Polymer page on GitHub:** https://github.com/Polymer/polymer

- **Polymer official documentation:** https://www.polymer-project. org/3.0/start/

- **Polymer channel on Slack:** https://polymer-slack.herokuapp.com/

- **Polymer on Google+:** http://plus.google.com/107187849809354688692/

That sums it up about Polymer! In the next chapter, we will be focusing on MeteorJS, another free, open source and isomorphic JS framework meant for rapid prototyping.

CHAPTER 5

Meteor

Carrying on from the previous chapter, in this one, we will be turning our attention to another popular JavaScript framework. With a tagline that loudly states "build apps with JavaScript," Meteor is quite possibly as straightforward about its job as a JavaScript framework can be.

But don't let a simple introduction fool you!

Meteor is a powerful and highly versatile JavaScript framework that is capable of handling complex projects of any size. It can work well and play along with custom components, such as React components, etc. Furthermore, it offers a very simple app structure, wherein we just modify client-side files separately, and server-side files separately.

Still need more? Meteor already has a proven track-record and has been used to build various popular and enterprise-ready applications.

INTRODUCTION

Now that we have established that Meteor is no minnow in the field of JavaScript frameworks, let us get started by first having an introductory look at Meteor in itself.

What Is Meteor?

In pure textbook terms, Meteor is a simple and open-source JavaScript framework meant for building dynamic and modern web applications. It supports the latest JavaScript coding standards and integrates well with popular open-source libraries.

DOI: 10.1201/9781003203711-5

Considering the fact that Meteor integrates with various other open-source libraries and frameworks, it is a good pick for a wide variety of uses. The learning curve in itself is not steep at all, and Meteor has a robust code base that can handle bigger projects with ease.

Meteor is often employed in big-scale commercial projects. Beyond that, React or Angular developers might often find Meteor to be simpler to learn, use and deploy, especially when used in sync with Angular or React components.

What Makes Meteor Special?

The Ultimate Selling Point of Meteor is its simple architecture and fairly straightforward mode of operation. The list of dependencies is virtually negligible, and Meteor even ships with npm thereby ensuring that environments that do not already have npm preinstalled can still make use of package installation via npm.

The catch is that in order to call the npm version bundled with Meteor, the command we will need to use is *meteor npm*

On the other hand, to call the global npm version (assuming we have it installed on our system), we simply need to use the command *npm*

The rest of the command and parameters remain the same. For example, to install lodash modules using the global npm command, we will issue:

```
npm install lodash --save
```

Whereas to install the same using the npm version bundled with Meteor, we will issue the command as follows:

```
meteor npm install lodash --save
```

But what exactly is the difference anyway? Well, if a given environment does not already have npm installed, it can save us a bit of time. Furthermore, using the bundled npm version is important if we are keen on adding Node.js modules that have binary dependencies and make native C calls (the bundled npm version, when used, can ensure that the modules are compiled using the same libraries).

But that is not the only thing that Meteor does differently. Another special aspect of Meteor is that it relies on an integrated JavaScript stack that can ensure we get a lot of execution done using the bare minimum lines of code. In other words, working with Meteor can save a good deal of time and also enhance the end user experience as we have full-fledged control over every aspect of the application.

Pros

The most obvious advantage associated with Meteor is its relative ease of use for the beginner-level developers. Even if we do not have npm on our system, or are unaware of complex installation procedures, Meteor is rather simplified in terms of setting up and installation.

Beyond that, Meteor lets us build a wide array of apps that can run across any nature of device. Be it iOS, Android, or desktop, Meteor apps can run seamlessly and perfectly well across all platforms.

We have already discussed how using Meteor can save both time and effort. In fact, due to its ease of use and less strain on development time, Meteor has become a popular name in the league of JavaScript frameworks within a short span of time. Companies such as QualComm and IKEA have turned to Meteor to develop and deploy versatile and robust web apps for their internal as well as client-facing platforms.

Another benefit that we can associate with Meteor is the fact that it integrates and plays well with various other libraries and JavaScript frameworks. Need to include a component from Angular or React? How about Blaze? Yes, Meteor supports them all! Meteor also integrates with the likes of MongoDB, Vue, and even Apache Cordova!

Cons

We have talked a good deal about the pros of Meteor, but are there any noticeable disadvantages?

For the most part, Meteor does not have a long list of downsides that developers tend to worry about. However, the lack of server-side rendering out of the box means the web application, in its final build, will not be very SEO-ready. Of course, we have the option of using custom plugins or adding server-side rendering from our end for Search Engine Optimization and speed-related purposes, but Meteor does not have any such feature natively built into it.

When building a complex app, there is very little scope to stick truly and only to Meteor. More often than not, developers tend to find themselves resorting to importing custom components and libraries and then use the same within Meteor. This, of course, is not much of a negative point, but is still something worth noting for the puritans at heart.

HOW TO USE?

Now that we have learned what Meteor.js is all about, let us see it in action. But before going further, we first need to install Meteor.js

Installing Meteor.js

Installing Meteor.js is fairly easy. At this stage, you might already be well-versed with installation of JavaScript frameworks. Therefore, Meteor installation too should not take much time for you to accomplish.

If you are a Windows user, you will need Chocolatey to install Meteor.js

Chocolatey is a dedicated package manager for developers working on the Windows OS. It comes with its own set of amazing features that help you automate software and package management as well as updates on Windows. You can use it to search for, install, upgrade and uninstall packages from the command line itself.[1]

After you have successfully installed Chocolatey, you can simply run the following command from the command prompt (with Administrator privileges, obviously):

```
choco install meteor
```

The rest will take care of itself.

On the other hand, if you are on Linux or Mac, you can fire up the command line terminal and then run the command as under—curl https://install.meteor.com/ | sh

Perchance we already have Meteor installed on our system, running the above curl command as superuser will remove the older version and install the latest Meteor version.

Unlike most of the other JavaScript frameworks that we have seen or will learn about in this book, Meteor.js comes with npm preloaded. So this means even if your system does not have npm, there is no need to install it separately.

Alternatively, should you prefer sticking with npm, you can continue using it to manage your projects and packages (in that case, you will need to have globally installed npm).

That is all that there is to installation of Meteor.js.

Upon successful installation, we will see a confirmation message.

---

[1] Learn more about Chocolatey for Windows at https://chocolatey.org/

Once we have successfully installed Meteor, it is time to start serving apps using it.

Serving an App in Meteor.js

Once we have installed Meteor.js we first need to create a project. This project in itself will be where the bulk of our development will happen.

To create a project, we need to:

```
meteor create myfancyapp
```

By running the above command, we are creating a project named myfancyapp.

Now, we are ready to run or serve the app locally. The following commands will accomplish the task for us.

```
cd myfancyapp
meteor npm install
meteor
```

Basically, we are first navigating to the directory of our project. Thereafter, we are running the app itself on localhost.

If everything goes as planned, the process in the terminal will show a success message.

Thereafter, we can simply navigate in our web browser to the displayed localhost address and our app is ready for viewing. Of course, it is still a barebones structure so there is not much to view, but the idea is clear.

At this stage, we have successfully launched and served our very first Meteor.js application! Now, how about we start doing something more with it?

Building Apps for the Web in Meteor

Creating apps in Meteor.js is fairly straightforward for the simple reason that this particular JavaScript framework is tailor-made for performance optimized web applications. As we have already discussed, Meteor.js has several features up its sleeve that make it perfect for developing and deploying progressive applications.

But in order to fully make use of Meteor's features, it is a good idea to first familiarize ourselves with the structure or organization of apps in Meteor.js.

In the previous section, we already learned how to creae a Meteor app. Let us repeat the command that we discussed earlier, assuming we are creating an app named MyFancyApp:

```
meteor create myfancyapp
```

The above command will create a directory named "myfancyapp" that will contain the files and code for our new application. To launch this app, we can execute the command in the app directory, as discussed above. The finalized code in the terminal, right from app creation to execution, should look something like this:

However, what does the structure or layout of a Meteor application really look like?

When we open the app directory, we will see the app structure with a root folder.

Most of these files are fairly self-explanatory.

The .meteor directory includes internal details for Meteor files. The package.json file, as we already are aware by now, includes details about npm packages.

In the server directory, we will come across a main.js file. This particular file serves as the starting point in JavaScript when loading on the server.

There is another main.js file, in the client directory. This one too serves as an entry point, but is loaded on the client-side.

The client directory also contains the main.html and main.css files— these are the ones that are rendered in the web browser.

Now, we know that we can just navigate to the app directory in a terminal and run the application using the *meteor* command.

Following that, we can simply open a web browser and head to http://localhost:3000 wherein our app will be loaded. We have already covered this in the previous section.

Wish to play around a bit? All we need to do is make HTML changes to the main.html file in the client directory, or add some fancy CSS to main.css file in the client directory itself. Once we save our changes, the http://localhost:3000 URL will be updated to reflect the same.

This automatic updating of the frontend display to reflect the changes in code is what we popularly refer to as Hot Reload! It is not an unheard concept in the world of JavaScript as more and more client-side frameworks support it nowadays, including Meteor.

So, what have we learned so far?

Our Meteor application structure is fairly simple. We can make HTML changes to the main.html file, or add another HTML file and import it therein. Similarly, CSS styling goes in the main.css file.

The main.js file is where we add all JavaScript code. If, by any chance, we need to import custom JavaScript scripts, such as React libraries or components, we can simply run the required npm command and that should suffice.

For the most part, this is all that there is to Meteor app development. Naturally, you will need to couple it with more detailed and possibly additional knowledge of JavaScript frameworks in order to build complex apps in Meteor. But now that you have a basic idea of how to set things up, it is fairly easier to take things forward.

CONCLUSION

Now that we have learned a basic bit of concepts related to Meteor, how do we take it forward?

The Meteor Ecosystem

Meteor, as a JavaScript framework, does not enjoy the fame and backing that is synonymous with certain other JavaScript frameworks. For example, while Angular has the backing of Google and React is loved by Facebook, Meteor does not have a corporate tech juggernaut full-time on its side.

With that said, it will probably be a huge mistake to assume that Meteor is not used and loved by bigger projects. There are various successful ventures and projects that have been built from the ground-up in Meteor.

It might be worthwhile to consider looking at projects such as Rocket. Chat or Telescope to further see what Meteor is capable of.

Beyond that, the Meteor community in itself is very helpful and rather active. If you are just getting started with Meteor, asking questions and getting answers will not be much of a trouble.

- **Rocket.Chat:** https://rocket.chat/

- **Telescope:** http://www.telescopeapp.org/

- **Wekan:** https://wekan.github.io/

Further Steps

As you get rolling with Meteor, you will soon notice that this particular JavaScript framework is meant for highly dynamic projects that definitely must have a client-facing environment.

In fact, for the most part, Meteor is a worthy option to consider when building or working on projects and applications that interact heavily with users—such as ticket booking solutions, news aggregator sites, viral content curation systems, etc.

In this effect, Meteor has uses that can serve rather popular and bigger projects. With that said, for the most part, one might find oneself often turning to additional JavaScript libraries or frameworks to use in assonance with Meteor.

This does not imply that Meteor cannot be used as a standalone Js framework. On the contrary, there are often requirements that make it essential to use the likes of React or Vue in a given project; thankfully, Meteor comes with npm bundled and installing a separate component or package is no big deal.

Suggested Resources

Finally, should you wish to learn further and delve deeper into the world of Meteor, where do you get started?

Well, the first place to start should ideally be the Meteor homepage at https://www.meteor.com/

Next, and quite possibly, the best and most frequently updated resource for Meteor is the official guide itself at https://guide.meteor.com/

And to stay updated with the development, or to fork the project itself, Meteor's GitHub repo can be found at https://github.com/meteor/meteor

If you are an existing Meteor developer or have had some experience with it, you might consider migrating to Meteor 1.7 in order to make use of the latest features and all that this framework has to offer. There is a very detailed and properly outlined migration guide available at https://guide. meteor.com/1.7-migration.html

Similarly, for folks looking for video content, there are video tutorials available on the official channel at https://www.youtube.com/user/ MeteorVideos

Meteor forums are fairly active too and the community is larger than what you'd find at most other JavaScript frameworks. This is mainly due to the fact that Meteor offers easy integration with most other JavaScript frameworks and also because of the fact that client-facing dynamic apps are a strong forte of Meteor. Check out the forums at https://forums.meteor.com/

And lastly, for the socially active and outgoing people, Meteor community does have a good number of meetups around the world. More details can be found at https://www.meetup.com/en-US/topics/meteor/

That brings us to the end of this chapter about Meteor JavaScript framework.

In the next chapter, we will be turning our attention toward Aurelia, a simple yet sophisticated JavaScript framework that is slowly but steadily rising in popularity. Unlike Meteor, Aurelia serves a predefined set of purposes and is more of a use-case centric JavaScript framework.

CHAPTER 6

Aurelia

In the previous chapter, we learned about Meteor and its various uses. Meteor is a rather popular JavaScript framework that is rising steadily in popularity. With its diverse set of features, that we saw in the previous chapter, it is obvious that Meteor has a lot to offer.

Moving on, in this chapter, we will be turning our attention toward another JavaScript framework that is not as popular as, say, React or Angular, but is rising in usage. This particular JavaScript framework too, just like Meteor, has a very impressive list of features to offer.

Meet Aurelia, a JavaScript client framework for web, mobile as well as desktop that has zero external dependencies.

In this chapter, we will be exploring Aurelia in depth and learning more about what it has to offer and where it can make the best use of it.

INTRODUCTION

As mentioned, Aurelia is a client framework that comes with no external dependencies per se. But what makes it special and what is it all about? Let's find out!

What Is Aurelia?

As a client framework, Aurelia is meant for end user or client-side usage. In other words, it is not something that you would use on the server-side, such as Node.js.

With that said, Aurelia focuses more on usability and ease of production. It is written in next-generation ECMAScript and integrates seamlessly with Web Components. This means creating customized HTML elements or adding custom attributes to existing elements is fairly easy and straightforward.

In fact, even a newbie JavaScript developer can get started with Aurelia in no time. The architecture in itself is simple to comprehend—instead of being a monolithic framework, Aurelia is composed of smaller task-focused modules. This makes customization and abstraction easier for the developers.

But the big question is, what is so special about Aurelia?

What Makes It Special?

The biggest point that can be put forth in favour of Aurelia is that it is written in next-generation ECMAScript and integrates with Web Components. Now, add to it the fact that Aurelia has no external dependencies, and you have an impressive JavaScript framework for use in web and mobile apps right out of the box.

Furthermore, Aurelia is built up of small modules that are task-focused. This means developers can pick and select modules as per their needs, thereby helping them build highly customizable applications for the web. There is hardly any bloatware when working with Aurelia.

More importantly, Aurelia supports two-way data binding, much like many other JavaScript frameworks that we have discussed in this book. However, Aurelia comes with its own extensible HTML compiler that can take care of not just data binding but also dynamic loading and batch rendering. As we will see in later sections of this chapter, creating and using custom attributes in Aurelia is a breeze.

The client-side router in Aurelia has its own dynamic route patterns. However, it is worth noting that many developers tend not to use a router but instead work with data-based user interface (UI) composition— Aurelia supports that as well. It is possible to make use of existing modular conventions in Aurelia or customize them to suit special needs.

All in all, Aurelia is something that can be used for building simple applications that require minimal setup. If your primary goal is to save development time and wish to avoid spending a lot of time and effort in setting things up, Aurelia might be the right fit. More importantly, when working or developing with Web Standards, Aurelia is a good choice for a JavaScript framework.

Pros

The biggest advantage that Aurelia can boast of is its broad language support. Irrespective of what you wish to use, be it ES5, ES 2015, ES 2016, or TypeScript, Aurelia can handle it all. All of its APIs are cross-compliant, which means there is seamless compatibility with many scripting languages.

Such compatibility also implies that ES 2015 and other modules can be used to write minimal code. More often than not, Aurelia projects and apps do not tend to span thousands of lines of code. This, of course, depends heavily on the size and magnitude of the project that we are dealing with, but minimally coupled code is the norm in Aurelia.

Beyond that, as we have already seen, Aurelia offers us the ability to create custom HTML elements. This means customization, tweaking and additional implementation is rather easy in Aurelia. With its small modules, we can take our pick and only opt for the ones that serve a specific purpose. Such a non-bloated approach gives Aurelia a simplicity that is often not found in bigger JavaScript frameworks.

Cons

On the downside, however, the option of choosing the custom modules that we need and omitting the ones that we do not need does not sit well with all users. At times, a monolithic JS framework is a good thing to have. Many developers, especially the ones not highly familiar with the world of JavaScript frameworks, do not want to piece modules together, but instead would prefer a monolithic structure that has very clearly-defined rules about what is allowed and what is not.

In such cases, Aurelia is often not the ideal pick. In fact, while Aurelia is rather easy to learn and even easier to master, its open-ended nature means it is equally easy to write poorly coded applications when working with Aurelia. It is highly advisable, especially for newer developers, to first hone their coding skills and adhere to the recommended standards in a framework such as Angular or React, and then turn to something like Aurelia. For someone absolutely unfamiliar with standardized coding methodology, Aurelia is too blank a canvas to be helpful.

Considering the fact that Aurelia is a client framework, it is often more geared toward front-end development. This, in itself, is surely not a disadvantage per se. But for folks looking for something that does more than just that, Aurelia is not a one-size-fits-all solution.

Well, that is enough theoretical introduction to Aurelia. How about we get started with it and see Aurelia in action?

HOW TO USE AURELIA?

Before getting started with actual usage, we first need to install Aurelia. The installation process in itself is fairly simple and, considering the fact that you are already familiar with the installation steps of several other JavaScript frameworks, installing Aurelia too should be no big deal.

Installing Aurelia

For the most part, you will be working with the Aurelia Command Line Interface (CLI). As such, Aurelia CLI is exactly what we will be installing. Depending on your environment, you may need to run the command as root or superuser, such as sudo on Linux. With that said, there are certain prerequisites to installing Aurelia CLI.

First up, we will need the latest version of Node.js. We will be covering Node.js at length later on during the course of this book. However, as we learned in the previous chapters too, Node.js is a server-side framework that is often required for running many other JavaScript frameworks. You can grab the latest version from the official website itself: https://nodejs.org/en/

Beyond that, we will also be needing a Git client. It is preferable to use the standard Git client from the https://git-scm.com/ website, which is available in a cross-platform manner, depending on the operating system of your choice. Perchance you wish to use a graphical interface desktop client, GitHub has one such option that can be accessed at https://desktop.github.com/

Once the Node.js and Git requirements are met, Aurelia CLI can be installed from the command line using npm. It must be noted that npm is installed alongside Node.js anyway. The command to install Aurelia CLI would be:

```
npm install aurelia-cli-g
```

The above command will install Aurelia CLI globally on our system.

It is often said that creating a new project does not need the latest version of npm and as such, even if a given system or setup does not have the latest version of Node.js, one can still go ahead with Aurelia installation and usage on an outdated npm version. In technical and literal terms, this is true to some extent. However, frontend development, in all practical purposes, requires flat-package structure and really outdated versions of npm cannot possibly support that. Thus, it is highly advisable, both from a logical as well as security perspective, to use the latest version of Node.js and npm.

Now that we have Aurelia CLI installed and ready for action, it is time to get started with app development!

Creating and Localizing Apps with Aurelia

The first step, obviously, is to create a new project. For that, we can run the command as follows:

```
au new
```

The above command presents us with a series of options and queries. For the uninitiated, this is where the project info is entered; first-time users of Aurelia can just stick to defaults, whereas advanced folks can opt for greater customization.

In either case, once the project is set up, Aurelia will fetch and install dependencies for use. Thereafter, we are free to get to work on our brand new project.

Once the project is setup, we can run the following command to execute the app:

```
au run
```

The above command will build the app, run the web server and then serve the application. As and when we make changes to the web app, the page itself will be refreshed too, as long as the web server is running.

For the most part, development in Aurelia can be accomplished via the Aurelia CLI as discussed above, especially for beginners. However, irrespective of the nature of the app that we are developing, it might be a good idea to consider localizing it at a later stage.

Therefore, it is wiser to add internationalization support as well. For that, we can turn to i18N config and support in Aurelia.

The first step, naturally, is to install the Aurelia i18n plugin in order to add internationalization and localization features to our app. This particular plugin comes with support for internationalization and can help us localize our app.

It goes without saying that we are going to need Node.js as well as npm in order to install the plugin. Beyond that, we will obviously need Aurelia CLI already setup and running, so as to make use of the plugin in our applications.

Once everything is setup, the installation can be accomplished using the following command:

```
npm install aurelia-i18n --save
```

It is worth noting that the Aurelia i18n plugin is optimized for both JavaScript and TypeScript usage. That said, the above command will proceed with the installation and the terminal might look something like the following:

Beyond that, it is also a good idea to install i18next and a backend loader of choice. Aurelia does come with its own backend loader, but i18next is advisable to be used irrespective of the backend plugin question.

Wondering what i18next is? Well, it is a simple and general-purpose open source library with a wide range of features. It is more of an internationalization framework meant for JavaScript coders and provides us with a standard set of i18n features. It can be used or integrated with various JavaScript frameworks as well as several other platforms. Naturally, i18next is a worthy choice for adding localization support to your apps and projects.

In Aurelia, the Aurelia-i18n plugin in itself uses i18next as its backbone for serving localized content. Considering the fact that i18next is fully scalable and versatile, the Aurelia-i18n plugin too inherits the same set of features and flexibility.

To install i18next, the following command will suffice:

```
npm install i18next - save
```

You can learn more about i18next at its homepage –https://www.i18next .com/

The last step will be to open the aurelia.json file of our app, and then add the following set of dependencies therein:

```
{
    "name": "i18next",
    "path": "../node_modules/i18next/dist/umd",
    "main": "i18next"
},
{
    "name": "aurelia-i18n",
    "path": "../node_modules/aurelia-i18n/dist/amd",
    "main": "aurelia-i18n"
}
```

That is all! We have added localization and internationalization support to our Aurelia app within minutes!

CONCLUSION

In this chapter, we have covered a fairly basic overview of Aurelia as a framework. We can build upon this knowledge to gain further mastery over Aurelia and do more with it.

The Aurelia Ecosystem

As a JavaScript client framework for web, mobile and desktop, Aurelia has a lot of potential to talk about. However, in terms of its ecosystem, newer users tend to encounter certain roadblocks.

The first and foremost consideration that needs to be borne in mind is that Aurelia's documentation is plain confusing at times. This makes the learning curve even steeper for the beginners. With that said, the community-run literature on the internet is fairly satisfactory, but the official documentation is rather badly segregated and one might struggle to locate key concepts quickly.

With all that said, learning Aurelia has several key advantages of its own. For the most part, it is a flexible framework that can adapt to a wide variety of usages. Whilst it does not enjoy as much popularity as, say, React, it is still a worthy choice for many developers and users. As such, if you are looking for a simple client framework that just gets the job done without any frills, Aurelia is surely deserving of a look!

Further Steps

Now that you have been introduced to Aurelia, what lies ahead?

It might be a good idea to take a few moments to familiarize yourself with the Aurelia workflow at large. There are several plugins and extensions that can make life easier for the Aurelia developers.

For the most part, you may find yourself turning toward Aurelia for building simplified web apps or similar projects. Even more importantly, you may also consider integrating it with Polymer or Webpack (we will cover Webpack later on during the course of this book), keeping in mind that Aurelia is both localization-ready and capable of handling external queries.

Suggested Resources

For the most part, Aurelia can be mastered without referring to a diverse array of literature.

- If you are looking for practical examples, there is a sample To Do application tutorial at https://aurelia.io/docs/tutorials/creating-a-todo-app and also Contact Manager app tutorial at https://aurelia.io/docs/tutorials/creating-a-contact-manager

- Beyond that, Aurelia has its own training section too, accessible at https://aurelia.io/#training address.

- Lastly, *Practical App Development with Aurelia* by Matthew Duffield is a good book to refer to should you seek a detailed guide for app development in Aurelia. This book can be accessed at https://www.apress.com/us/book/9781484234013

- Aurelia Homepage: https://aurelia.io/home

This brings us to the end of this chapter about Aurelia. So far, we have learned about six different JavaScript frameworks.

In the next chapter, we will be turning our attention toward Svelte, that is a JavaScript framework meant to create frameworkless apps—confused? Let's discover more about Svelte in the next chapter!

CHAPTER 7

Svelte

In the previous chapter, we learned about the Aurelia JavaScript framework. Much like all other frameworks in JavaScript, Aurelia too is required to be loaded and run during the execution of the code. But will it not be nicer if a given framework provides you with templates that are, technically, framework-less?

Wondering how is that possible?

In this chapter, we will be covering one such JavaScript framework that can do just that. Svelte, the JS framework under discussion, describes itself as a "magical disappearing user interface (UI) framework." This particular phrase in itself is clear enough to tell us that Svelte is meant for UI development.

Of course, that is not sufficient to justify Svelte's advantages and purpose. So let us get started with a more thorough introduction to this nimble and versatile JavaScript framework.

INTRODUCTION

We will first be discussing the benefits and advantages, as well as any possible drawbacks that Svelte brings to the table. Thereafter, we will get down to installation and actual usage of the framework.

What Is Svelte?

As mentioned above, Svelte uses the tagline "the magical disappearing UI framework." When we say "disappearing," we mean that term rather

DOI: 10.1201/9781003203711-7

pragmatically—Svelte converts our apps into pure JavaScript at build time, not at run time.

Now What Would That Mean?

Well, let us put it this way. In the previous chapters of this book, we have read about JS frameworks such as React, Angular, Vue, and others. Most of them tend to have one common trait, irrespective of the purpose they are used for—such JS frameworks help us write our code with ease, and then convert or interpret the application code into ideal JS as and when the code is run or executed.

Naturally, this implies the JS framework in itself needs to stick around for the run time. Svelte, on the other hand, converts the application code into ideal JS at build time itself. This means we do not really need to tag along Svelte in its entirety at the run time.

In easiest of terms, instead of shipping a gigantic run time, Svelte is compiled at build time. This leaves us with a reduced file size for our code and an inherently optimized application.

What Makes Svelte Special?

The most obvious as to why Svelte is special is its ability to generate framework-less and highly reduced code.

By and large, considering the fact that we have already covered a good number of JS frameworks so far, we are aware that most frameworks tend to require us to add them to our pages as <script> tags.

However, Svelte is slightly different. Keeping in mind that Svelte does not execute at run time, but instead it runs at build time, we need to integrate it in our build systems.

Depending on the build system of our choice, be it Rollup or Gulp or likewise, we can find the required plugin of choice and then integrate Svelte accordingly. Later on in this chapter, we will cover REPL and Rollup integration at length, and also discuss the links to plugins related to various other build systems for integrating Svelte.

This is exactly where the uniqueness and speciality of Svelte lies. By requiring integration with the build system itself, Svelte can provide the developers with greater and more comprehensive control. Furthermore, it does not require us to reinvent the wheel or modify our manner of working, but instead, Svelte moulds itself accordingly depending on the plugin and build system that we choose to integrate it with.

With that said, it is also noteworthy that Svelte offers a good deal of speed and execution improvements. There is little or no need to bundle bulky dependencies with our code and cause run time delays; Svelte tackles everything way ahead of that at build time.

In this effect, it will probably not be a wrong deduction if we were to call Svelte more of a compiler in its own right, with the prowess and abilities of a JS framework for UI development. Considering the viewpoint that Svelte compiles during the build process, it does have a lot in common with modern-day compilers.

Pros

The biggest and most obvious advantage that Svelte has to offer is the fact that it converts the app into ideal JS at build time and therefore, there is no bloatware during run time. This comparatively reduces the load time, giving us apps that are not just smaller in size but also faster to load.

Naturally, since load time comes down, it is only but obvious that memory usage of the application is rather less as well. Svelte almost eliminates the overhead of having a runtime library, thereby giving us JS code that is better optimized, cleaner to execute, easier to run and consumes lesser memory resources.

But Svelte saves a lot more than just execution time! By giving us reusable blocks of code that encapsulate mutually related functions and features (called Components), Svelte can save a good deal of development time as well. This means our apps can not only run faster, but also be built faster!

Svelte has an API of its own for folks that prefer a neat and logical developmental workflow. It is easy to install (as well shall soon see in this chapter) and even easier to learn. Furthermore, Svelte can integrate seamlessly with an existing project code base and further enhance the code run time.

This means Svelte is a good option for not just standalone development but also for integration into existing and larger projects. With that said, Svelte's single file components and faster processing make it a worthy option for building mobile apps too, such as Android applications.

Cons

But Svelte cannot be all amazing now, can it?

The biggest downside of Svelte is that it is still a less popular entity when it comes to the league of JS frameworks. Sure, it is rising at a praiseworthy rate and boasts of some amazing performance improvements, at the end of the day, Svelte is not the highly popular JS framework that one might expect it to be.

At the time of writing, Svelte's Discord channel has a little over 550 users in total; this is a good enough number for most folks, but if the expectation is to look for thousands of active users, Svelte is going to appear too small.

Even more so, keeping in mind that Svelte has an approach that is rather unique, it may or may not find a place in everyone's workflow. If you are not comfortable integrating a JS framework within the build system and would rather prefer something that is mainstream, Svelte is probably not the ideal pick for you.

The documentation is praiseworthy, indeed. However, it is still far from what one might expect in terms of user-friendliness; there are no video tutorials or separate step by step guides for the beginner-level users. However, Svelte is still just getting started, so things are certainly going to improve over the course of time.

For now, keeping in view that Svelte has a lot of possibilities and is a rather impressive JS framework, it is highly advisable to spend some time getting to know it better and more closely.

And for that, let us get started with the usage of Svelte!

HOW TO USE SVELTE?

Now that we have understood just what Svelte can do for us, let us get started with its usage.

Installing Svelte

The first step toward using any JS framework is, obviously, the installation! So far, for the most part, we have been using npm to install JS framework. When it comes to Svelte too, the same can potentially be applied. Svelte is available in the npm package repo over at https://www.npmjs.com/package/svelte and comes with detailed installation and usage guidelines.

For the most part, our command to install Svelte via npm will be:

```
npm install svelte
```

Other than that, much like Aurelia, Svelte too has its own Command Line Interface (CLI) that we can install and make use of. To install the Svelte CLI globally, we can use the following command:

```
npm install -g svelte-cli
```

Now, we have installed Svelte and Svelte CLI via npm, so it is safe to assume that everything is ready for work? Well, apparently not.

In general, the Svelte CLI is very useful if we are only trying to give Svelte a first try to see what it might be capable of, and how it functions. But if the end goal is serious-minded application development, the Svelte CLI is not recommended.

For production usage, the Svelte CLI can surely compile our components with ease, but it does not automatically recompile the components as and when changes are made. This means each time we make a change to our code, the compilation process will have to be repeated manually. This pretty much defeats the purpose of using a JS framework where the goal is to save time and efforts.

As a result, while we can surely give the Svelte CLI a spin whenever we want to, for production usage, we might be in need of something much faster and easier.

And for that very purpose, let us turn our attention toward Svelte REPL.

Building Apps with Svelte

The easiest way to get started with Svelte is not via the CLI. Instead, we can head over to Svelte REPL, that is located at https://svelte.technology/repl

The Svelte REPL contains a list of handy examples for beginner-level users. If you are just beginning with Svelte development, perhaps it might be a good idea to go through the examples at large.

Now, the best part about the REPL is that we can start off with some basic coding straightaway and preview the changes and HTML therein. Once we are confident that our code has outgrown the Svelte REPL, all we need to do is hit the Download button to grab a zip file containing all of the relevant code files.

Once downloaded, we can unzip the file to any directory of our choice. Thereafter, in the terminal window, we need to navigate to the said directory:

```
cd my/directory/path/svelte-app
```

And run npm install therein:

```
npm install
```

Followed in turn by running the dev engine:

```
npm run dev
```

This will launch our app and the engine will be waiting for changes, as shown in the terminal window.

We can safely navigate to the localhost: 5000 port address in the web browser of our choice. Furthermore, as and when we make changes to our code files (located in the src sub-directory within the app directory), the output will be refreshed to show the latest changes.

This is it! We have Svelte setup and running on our development system, and we can start building awesome stuff with it.

Understanding Svelte Components

In Svelte, components are the building blocks of every application. Thus, we can say that a Svelte component is a reusable self-contained code block that brings together styles, markup and other assets of one group.

In the practical world, every component that we come across will be a single HTML file. Then, Svelte can transform each HTML file into a JS module that can further be imported into our application.

For instance, say we have a component residing at something.html

Now, to use this component which is just a single file, we will import it into our application, such as:

```
import Cmp from './something.html';
const xyz = new Cmp({
        target: document.querySelector('main'),
        data: { name: 'world' }
});
```

The above code will import the component. We can then modify its data, for instance:

```
xyz.set({ name: 'planet' });
```

And when the application has run its course, we can detach the component and clean up the memory:

```
xyz.destroy();
```

That's all for components! The above example shows you how Svelte API works in practical usage. It might be worth the effort to learn more about the available Components API in Svelte, as the list is often updated to reflect the newer changes: https://svelte.technology/guide#component-api

Additional Info: Using degit to Scaffold the Svelte Template

Keeping in mind that Svelte is primarily meant for UI development, it is natural for developers to be curious about the frontend of their applications.

In essence, each time we download a zip file from Svelte REPL and start working on it on our system, we are also grabbing a customized version of the Svelte template.

This particular template, in itself, can be found over at GitHub at https://github.com/sveltejs/template

For the most part, many developers might prefer customizing the template to suit their requirements and needs. In such cases, forking the template makes good sense and can easily be done on GitHub. However, do we really need to tinker with zip files all the time?

This is where degit can come into play. It is a simple, fully open source and entirely free to use project scaffolding tool. In other words, degit can be used to make copies of existing Git repositories. Thus, when we run degit repo-address-here, it locates the latest commit to the said repository, and then downloads the tar file.

degit GitHub repository can be found at https://github.com/Rich-Harris/degit

degit in itself is fairly faster than using git clone as we will not be downloading the entire Git history, only the latest commit as a tar.gz file.

In order to use degit with Svelte, the first step is to install degit. We will need Node.js and npm on our system, and then the following command can do the trick for us:

```
npm install -g degit
```

Then, we can safely download the latest commit from the Svelte template:

```
degit sveltejs/template mysvelteapp2
```

After that, the process is same as above, wherein we will first navigate to the app directory:

```
cd mysvelteapp2
```

And then run the install command:

```
npm install
```

It is worth noting that degit works by default with directories on our local disks that are empty. Perchance the directory is not empty, we will need to either use a new directory, or specify override options to degit (this can be found in the degit official guide). Here is what our command line or terminal may look like:

This can then be followed by starting the dev engine:

```
npm run dev
```

The default template will show us Hello World! in the browser. And the dev engine will display the progress accordingly in the terminal.

Once the app is ready, we can safely run the build command:

```
npm run build
```

Svelte comes with detailed instructions on how to deploy the applications to Surge and other services.

The code from the above example can be found in the book's code files sections. The final build can be found in the/public directory.

The above app, of course, is just a blank canvas template that shows Hello World, but on the basis of this model, we can build more complex apps.

Furthermore, whilst we have followed Rollup and REPL in the above example, Svelte comes with various other integrations of its own, including one for Webpack. We will be turning to Webpack later in the course of this book. If you are wondering about integrations with other build systems, here is a list of the relevant plugins:

- **gulp-svelte:** Gulp plugin

- **metalsmith-svelte:** Metalsmith plugin

- **system-svelte:** System.js plugin

- **svelte-loader:** Webpack plugin

- **meteor-svelte:** Meteor plugin

- **sveltejs-brunch:** Brunch plugin
- **rollup-plugin-svelte:** Rollup plugin
- **parcel-plugin-svelte:** Parcel plugin
- **sveltify:** Browserify plugin

CONCLUSION

In this chapter, we have learned a fair deal about Svelte. We now know that Svelte, as a frontend UI framework, is fairly different in its mode of operation from other existing frameworks.

To put it in easier words, we have seen how Svelte differs from various other JS frameworks, such as its functionality as a compiler, how we'd rather prefer working with a build system than a CLI, and so on.

The Svelte Ecosystem

Svelte is still a minnow in comparison to the likes of Angular, React, or Vue. As such, it is rather too much to expect a large community base surrounding it.

With that said, Svelte's USP is its ability to reduce the code size in practice. Since it compiles stuff at build time, Svelte is earning a reputation for its speed and optimization abilities. More importantly, Svelte can help organizations and coders save a lot of performance cost and time for their applications.

This is precisely why Svelte can make a worthy JS framework of choice for many apps where speed and execution is of essence.

In other words, while one may not opt for building an entire project with Svelte as a standalone framework, it is a very good idea to consider adding Svelte incrementally to an existing code setup. Furthermore, Svelte Components can easily be shipped as standalone packages that can function sans dependencies in most cases.

Naturally, assuming you already have an existing code base at hand, Svelte can be integrated therein to reduce the final build size as well as execution time. Perchance you have not already done so, it is well worth giving a serious thought.

Further Steps

As mentioned above, Svelte can be used to enhance the performance and reduce the code size of your existing applications. With that said, while we have followed the REPL model in this chapter, you can consider opting for the methodology that fits your model the best.

For instance, you can integrate with Webpack, Browserify or stick to the Svelte CLI (in spite of its issues, the CLI does work for many experienced coders), or just head over to the Svelte API and make calls to the API directly from within your app.

It is worth noting that the Svelte community, albeit small, is proactive and should you build something fun with Svelte, it is recommended to share it with the community's Svelte Gitter chatroom at https://gitter.im/sveltejs/svelte

The Svelte community Discord is fairly new but might be worth a try as well: https://discord.gg/yy75DKs

Suggested Resources

For the most part, the official documentation is a good place to start, though it still may seem like a work in progress for folks who are accustomed to richer documentation.

With that said, when working on complex apps, the API is worth referring to at https://github.com/sveltejs/svelte#api

Other than that, some other useful links are as follows:

- Svelte Homepage: https://svelte.technology/

- Documentation: https://svelte.technology/guide

- GitHub: https://github.com/sveltejs/svelte

- Svelte REPL: https://svelte.technology/repl

This brings us to the end of this chapter about Svelte. As a simple UI framework that prides itself in its unique approach and compiling abilities, Svelte is surely something you should look at especially if you are serious about JS frameworks that care about optimization and performance.

Svelte's "framework without a framework" has been appealing to a lot of people lately, and it will not be a surprise if Svelte were to rise in popularity at a rapid pace in times to come.

For now, that should suffice for our discussion on Svelte.

In the next chapter, we will be turning our attention toward another simple, small yet useful JS framework that offers easy to use and context-aware JS modules—Conditioner.js

CHAPTER 8

Conditioner.js

In the previous chapter, we learned about Svelte, an easy-to-use JavaScript framework that focuses on performance and optimization and can enhance run time speed of our apps.

In this chapter, going forward, we will be discussing another useful and very handy JavaScript framework that cares about speed and performance. Meet Conditioner.js—a JavaScript framework that is especially meant for content-based websites. If your website requires some interactive functionality and you really care about user experience, Conditioner. js might just be made for you!

But what makes this JavaScript framework special and why should we bother with it? Isn't web development already complicated enough with a plethora of frameworks out there? What can Conditioner.js do to solve problems?

Yes, this chapter will answer all of the above queries as we explore Conditioner.js in greater detail.

INTRODUCTION

Conditioner.js describes itself as a JavaScript framework that provides "frizz free, context-aware, JavaScript modules" for developers.

Naturally, since we are talking about modules, we need to comprehend what exactly Conditioner.js is attempting to accomplish.

DOI: 10.1201/9781003203711-8

What Is Conditioner.js?

Simply put, Conditioner.js is a JavaScript framework meant for content-oriented websites. When we say content-oriented, we mean modern day websites that focus on content publication or work with different forms of data and information. This can include virtually any website that we may think of, such as Wikipedia, Apress.com and likewise.

The end goal behind Conditioner.js is to enhance the presentational aspects of websites with the help of JavaScript, thereby offering a better and enhanced user experience.

This, of course, can go a long way in making our websites more presentable as well as more flexible. At the very least, Conditioner.js makes full use of functional JavaScript elements, thereby giving us the ability to leverage greater functionality out of such elements.

What Makes Conditioner.js Special?

Simply by describing its major purpose as providing "frizz free, context-aware, JavaScript modules" does not really imply Conditioner.js is well worth the time, does it? There are various smaller and minnow-sized JavaScript frameworks out there that are here today and gone tomorrow. Naturally, any sane developer might be apprehensive about the practical implementation and long run viability of using Conditioner.js in commercial or enterprise projects, especially highly diverse applications.

But this is precisely what makes Conditioner.js special for us. Unlike many other JavaScript frameworks, Conditioner.js does not focus on building web applications.

Yes, you read that right.

Conditioner.js is highly aimed toward content-aware "websites," and is not something we can use for building content-aware "web apps."

One might wonder, is there really that much of a difference? In today's world, "websites" and "web apps" are used almost interchangeably and a good number of folks in the developer community may not see much of a difference between the two. Furthermore, any decent and properly-structured website can be converted to a web app with ease, and with the rise of progressive enhancements, more and more interactive websites are heading toward the territory of web apps.

Conditioner.js goes a step further and describes "websites" as something that is created from a content point of view. The goal behind websites, therefore, is to serve content to the users.

Now, since we are focusing mostly on the content, anything that is done on the website should revolve around the content:

- Semantic HTML is required to describe the content itself, not the other way round.

- CSS is used to make the content presentable across various screen sizes and browser specifications.

- JavaScript, similarly, is used to provide a better user experience when working with the content, such as animations, clickable buttons, selectable values in forms, etc.

As can be seen, our definition of "websites," as per Conditioner.js, is fairly broad. Any content-serving website can fit the bill here.

- Wikipedia? Yes.

- The Apress site? Yes.

- Newspaper sites? Yes.

- Your college site? Again yes.

What does not fit the above definition includes the likes of email web apps, Google Maps, and so on. These, ideally, are "web apps" and not something Conditioner.js may be able to help with.

The above distinction, in all honesty, is a fair deal of nitpicking. Most of the "web apps" too tend to work with content—in fact, there is hardly anything on the web that does not utilize content. Conditioner.js argues that "web apps" such as a maps' or email client tends to "interact" with content, whereas websites tend to "present" content.

This is the bottleneck. If a given project is focused on presenting content, we can classify it as a website and Conditioner.js can be considered. If, on the other hand, we are interacting or utilizing content, we have a web app at hand and Conditioner.js should rather be avoided.

Now, since Conditioner.js focuses solely on websites, it can be argued that the goal here is to enhance the overall presentational aspects of JavaScript.

Pros

Having something such as Conditioner.js that is primarily dedicated toward creating a better experience for users serves one obvious purpose—we can improve the overall functioning and presentation of our website.

Most JavaScript modules tend to load rather quickly, as long as they are well optimized, properly coded and structured. Conditioner.js provides us with a form of progressive enhancement. It links JavaScript modules to DOM elements, on the basis of various parameters such as the size of the viewport, element visibility, and so on.

This implies Conditioner.js is a good pick when working with responsive design websites.

Furthermore, Conditioner.js is fairly easy to use and can be called as a script directly via Content Delivery Network (CDN). Switching existing websites to Conditioner.js is easy too.

Thus, ease of use, support for responsive web design as well as the ability to provide context-aware modules are some of the biggest positive aspects of Conditioner.js.

Cons

The biggest downside associated with Conditioner.js is the fact that it is a rather smaller JavaScript framework that has a very niche target audience. A good number of JavaScript developers tend to work with both web apps and websites. Relying on Conditioner.js means there may arise a need to maintain two separate sets of workflows—Conditioner.js is just not meant for web applications and developers will need to come up with a different set of frameworks for web app development. As such, the scope of use for Conditioner.js is very limited.

Even more so, content-aware websites are now rapidly being supplemented by applications, and the boundary between the two is fairly blurred as well. What do we do with a content publishing website that also offers stock trading, email or maps-like functionality? We selectively use Conditioner.js on pages that can find use for it?

As is obvious, unless the target project is custom-made for Conditioner.js, this particular JavaScript framework may not be able to justify its usage or inclusion in the first place. This pretty much guarantees that Conditioner. js will never achieve unmeasurable growth.

Furthermore, Conditioner.js does not have a gigantic community behind it. As it turns out, this JavaScript framework is mostly a one-man show, with certain other contributors in the mix. Enterprise-level usage may not be feasible for Conditioner.js where security fixes, updates and other active methods of development are often used to assess the viability and suitability of a given JavaScript framework.

With all of that said and done, Conditioner.js is a useful entity that can save our time in development.

HOW TO USE CONDITIONER.JS?

Let us now see Conditioner.js in action.

Installing Conditioner.js

Getting started with Conditioner.js is rather easy. We first need to install it, and the same can be accomplished via npm, pretty much like many other JavaScript frameworks that we have seen so far.

The command to install Conditioner.js via npm is as follows:

```
npm install conditioner-core --save
```

The default Conditioner.js package, as installed via npm, includes both the developmental and production versions. For production usage, the conditioner-core.min.js one will suffice.

However, the far easier and more straightforward method of using Conditioner.js is to do so via CDN using unpkg. We can simply include the script tag as follows:

```
<script src="https://unpkg.com/conditioner-core/
conditioner-core.js"></script>
```

That's all, Conditioner.js has now been added to our web page. Seems fairly easy, alright?

Using Conditioner.js

By default, Conditioner.js scripts behave pretty much like a for-loop. This means Conditioner.js will search for elements on the page that have the data-module attribute. Next, it will link the said elements to JavaScript functions having global scope.

In order to accomplish that, we first need to call the hydrate method:

```
<script src="https://unpkg.com/conditioner-core/
conditioner-core.js"></script>
<script>

// mounting modules
conditioner.hydrate( document.docElement );

</script>
```

Now that we have passed the docElement to hydrate method, Conditioner. js will selectively look through the page for data-module attribute and then bind it to global functions.

Following that, we are free to export functions as modules when working with our code. Conditioner.js comes with configurable options for both ES modules as well as Webpack and even AMD modules. This means if we do not wish to use Conditioner.js globally, the options are plenty!

It might be a good idea to get rolling with the boilerplate for the particular project setup or structure that you might be aiming for:

- **ES Modules**

- **Webpack**

- **Browserify**

- **AMD**

Adding Plugins to Conditioner.js

In Conditioner.js we can make use of plugins for additional functionality. Basically, the goal is to override internal methods or perhaps add some custom monitors to Conditioner.js using plugins.

Adding plugins to Conditioner.js is fairly easy and can be accomplished rather quickly. For this purpose, we can make use of the addPlugin method. It is noteworthy that this method expects a plugin definition object.

Beyond that, plugins in Conditioner.js can be linked to various hooks for added compatibility and performance.

Let us now take up the case of adding a plugin to Conditioner.js

In general, we are adding modules or referencing them by providing the full file name, such as filename.ext wherein ext refers to the extension. Now, let us say we wish to save the unnecessary work and automatically append the extension, such as .js when referencing module names.

We can make use of a plugin and then employ the moduleSetName hook to accomplish this. Here is how it might look:

```
conditioner.addPlugin({
moduleSetName: name => '${name}.js'
});
```

Now, whenever referencing a module, we can safely omit the extension and our plugin will add it automatically.

Conditioner.js comes with a list of custom hooks and filters that can be used in conjunction with plugins.

CONCLUSION

This brings us to the end of this chapter about Conditioner.js.

Keeping in mind that Conditioner.js is a very niche JavaScript framework with a highly focused usage and purpose, it is only obvious that there is not a lot to discuss here.

Conditioner.js Ecosystem

Conditioner.js is primarily about making smaller changes to the workflow and the way modules are loaded so as to enhance the overall page performance and speed. In the world of web development, such optimization techniques can obviously go a long way in boosting the overall growth of the website.

Naturally, the ecosystem is fairly small and the community size is not gigantic to talk about. However, Conditioner.js is entirely different from what one might expect from other JavaScript frameworks—there are web apps or mobile apps to be built using this particular framework. Naturally, the community in itself cannot be as loud as one might expect from other frameworks. Conditioner.js is something one would use to enhance and improve their website development workflow, and that is pretty much the end of the story.

For the most part, you can find Conditioner.js boilerplates as well as information related to plugins and hooks over at GitHub.

Further Steps and Suggested Resources

Rick Schennink, the developer behind Conditioner.js, has written a fairly detailed guide explaining the logic, purpose and goal behind Conditioner.js as well as talking a bit about the mode of operation of this JavaScript framework. It might be well worth the effort to read the same over at https://www.smashingmagazine.com/2018/03/lazy-loading-with-conditioner-js/

Beyond that, Conditioner.js is an active entity on GitHub, and for the most part, that is where the forking and activity happens.

- **Conditioner.js on GitHub:** https://github.com/rikschennink/conditioner/

- **Conditioner.js Homepage:** https://pqina.nl/conditioner/

For now, that sums up our discussion about Conditioner.js.

In the next chapter, we will be turning our attention toward Webix which happens to be another JavaScript framework for user interface (UI) development. However, this one comes with its own set of custom UI widgets as well as several CSS and HTML5 components to speed up the web development workflow.

CHAPTER 9

Webix

In the previous chapter, we learned about Conditioner.js which happens to be a JS framework meant solely for website development. Conditioner. js is a rather interesting concept in its own right albeit it cannot be used for a lot of purposes, especially when it comes to web-based applications.

In this chapter, we will be carrying on to discover another JS framework. More importantly, this one goes a step further and comes loaded with a range of modules, components and elements that can aid in user interface (UI) development.

Webix is a JS framework that comes with several HTML5 UI components and many feature-rich widgets. With that said, before going any further, it is also worth noting that Webix also has a premium variant.

So, paying for a JS framework? Does it make sense, especially with several amazing JS frameworks out there that are totally free to use and considerably more feature-rich and advanced than Webix?

Sure, these are all valid queries and depending whom you ask, you will get different answers, ranging from positive to negative. However, there is nothing wrong in having a business model as long as the said model is viable and the product has features and offerings to back it up.

This brings us to another question: does Webix really justify its premium offerings? In other words, is Webix worth the effort?

In order to answer all of these questions and more, we first need to familiarize ourselves with Webix and what it has to offer, what it can do for us, and more!

So without wasting anymore time, let us get started with Webix!

DOI: 10.1201/9781003203711-9

WHAT IS WEBIX?

In practical terms, Webix defines itself as a JavaScript UI framework for speeding up web development. Obviously, this definition is fairly broad. Let us take a moment to better understand what Webix really is.

Introducing Webix

Webix comes loaded with several skins and widgets that we can make use of in our projects. Thus, we can use Webix to save development time by using its UI elements, components and widgets instead of building everything from the ground up.

This implies that Webix is less of a coding mechanism and more of a conglomerate or combination of User Interface elements for web developers. Naturally, this can find many takers as a good number of web developers tend to waste precious time coding UI elements that can otherwise be found in the Webix library.

On the other hand, Webix does not seem to have much use for someone, say, a student of JavaScript or someone wanting to get to the detailed insights related to code. Webix is meant for professional developers, agencies and companies that know exactly what they intend to do with its libraries and widgets.

Now that we have established the real purpose and goal of Webix, what exactly does it have to offer and why should we be bothered with Webix? Let's read on to find out!

What Makes Webix Special?

Webix, as a JS framework, is fairly different from the others that we have covered in this book so far. At the very onset, it is evident from the fact that Webix comes with its own library of widgets that are "readymade" in nature—all we need to do is make use of them in our projects. Such widgets range from the very obvious, such as charts and maps, to highly complicated ones such as spreadsheet tables, graphs, and more.

Naturally, Webix is more of a "product" bundled as a JS framework. This is why having a premium variation for Webix makes good sense.

With that said, is Webix an entirely paid commodity? Definitely not.

Webix also has a free version that is fully open source and can be downloaded with ease. However, the free version lacks some of the advanced and highly feature-rich widgets that come loaded with the premium version. Furthermore, the paid plans come with support as well.

In this essence, Webix is fairly comparable to the world of WordPress plugins such as WooCommerce or likewise, wherein the core product is open source and free. However, with paid addons and modules, the basic functionality can be extended further.

In fact, Webix, as a combined library of UI components, is more of a geared and concentrated approach that many developers will find useful if they are aiming to save some time and quickly put together projects.

This may, very well, remind the readers of tools such as Bootstrap that are meant for saving development time as well. This is where the special and unique aspects of Webix are to be found—it is a collected assortment of resources that are production-ready and have been thoroughly tested for web development.

Features of Webix

- Easy to learn. The documentation is quite detailed, and it is not difficult to understand how everything works. You don't need to be a JS guru or a JS ninja to get started. You don't even need to understand the difference between them.

- Integration with popular frameworks. Implemented integration with Backbone.js, AngularJS, and jQuery. The latter feature, for example, allows you to create Webix widgets using jQuery syntax.

- Integration with third-party widgets. At this point, we will limit ourselves to the list: Mercury, Nicedit, Tinymce, CodeMirror, CKEditor, Raphael, D3, Sigma, JustPage, Google Maps, Nokia Maps, Yandex Maps, dhtmlxScheduler, and dhtmlxGantt.

- The size is small, the speed is high. In a compressed form. The js file weighs only 128 KB, and at the same time everything works quite quickly (according to the developers, it "flies" at all).

- Touch screen support. The created widgets feel equally good on both desktops and smartphones/tablets.

INSTALLATION AND USAGE

Now that we have learned what Webix is and what all it has to offer, let us get started with Webix development. The first step, obviously, is to install Webix.

Installing Webix

For the most part, we will be assuming that we are working with the open source and fully free version of Webix. The easiest and most direct way to install Webix is via the Content Delivery Network, or Content Delivery Network (CDN).

When using the CDN, we just need to specify the links to the webix.js and webix.css files located in the Webix CDN. In that case, here is how the specifications of our files may look like:

```
<!DOCTYPE HTML>
<html>
    <head>
    <link rel="stylesheet" href="https://cdn.webix.
com/edge/webix.css" type="text/css">
    <script src="https://cdn.webix.com/edge/webix.js"
type="text/javascript"></script>
    </head>
    <body>
        <script type="text/javascript"
charset="utf-8">

    // code comes here
        </script>
    </body>
</html>
```

The second option is to install via npm. We have already seen how to install several JS frameworks using npm and Webix is no different. The command is rather simple:

```
npm install webix
```

And the installation process with begin thereafter.

It is worth noting that when working with the premium version of Webix, npm installation is a good choice. While the above command is meant for the free open source version, the premium version commands can be found in the Webix documentation—generally, you'd need to specify your credentials so as to authenticate yourself as a licensed user.

There is a third method of installing Webix as well, albeit this is less of installation and more of downloading it. Once we have downloaded the free version of Webix, we can simply unzip the file and then refer to the required files in our code with relative paths.

In that case, our above example might appear something like this:

```
<!DOCTYPE HTML>
<html>
    <head>
        <!- Webix CSS file->
        <link rel="stylesheet" href="url/comes/here/
codebase/webix.css" type="text/css">
        <!- Webix JS file->
        <script src="url/comes/here/codebase/webix.js"
type="text/javascript"></script>
    </head>
    <body>
        <script>
        // app code
        </script>
    </body>
</html>
```

And that's all! We have now seen three different methods using which we can install and make use of Webix in our projects. Depending on our requirements and usages, we can opt for the Webix installation method that best suits our needs.

CONCLUSION

This brings us to the end of this chapter about Webix. To sum it up, Webix is a JavaScript framework that allows you to create desktop and mobile web applications with a responsive design. The framework is available under two licenses: GNU GPLv3 and commercial. Companies using Webix UI in product development are Toyota, Tesla, Mazda, Toshiba, Yamaha, Samsung, Fujitsu, and Siemens.

As such, we have now taken a look at numerous JS frameworks. In the next chapter, we will be turning our attention toward some common and very useful Node tools and libraries.

CHAPTER 10

Useful JavaScript Libraries and Tools

In the previous chapters, we covered some common and highly useful Node.js frameworks. Now, let us turn our attention to useful JavaScript libraries and tools. First, let us get started with task managers.

WHAT IS A TASK MANAGER?

Task Manager is a small application that is used to automate boring and routine, but no less important, tasks that you have to constantly perform during the project development process. Such tasks include, for example, running unit tests, file concatenation, minification, and CSS preprocessing. By simply creating a task file, you can instruct the task manager how to perform a particular task. And after that, you can go about your business. A fairly simple idea, which saves a lot of time, and helps to keep the focus on the tasks directly related to the development of the project.

NPM

Node.js allows you to write JavaScript applications on the server. It's built on the V8 JavaScript runtime and written in C++. It was primarily meant to be a server-side environment for applications, but developers have started using it to create tools to help them automate local tasks. Since then, a whole new ecosystem of Node-based tools has emerged to change the face of the front end.

DOI: 10.1201/9781003203711-10

To use these tools (or packages) in Node.js, we should be able to install them and manage them in a useful way. This is where npm, the Node package manager, comes in. It installs the packages you want to use and provides a user-friendly interface for working with them.

npm is a package manager that is part of Node.js. For many years, Node has been widely used by JavaScript developers to exchange tools, install various modules, and manage their dependencies. That's why for people working with Node.js, it is very important to understand what npm is.

npm was originally created as a package management system for Node. js, but nowadays it is also used in the development of frontend projects in JavaScript. To interact with the npm registry, the team of the same name is used, which gives the developer a huge number of opportunities.

How npm Works?

It works by performing one of its two roles:

1. It is a widely used repository for publishing Node projects.js is open source. This means that it is an online platform where everyone can publish and share tools written in JavaScript.

2. npm is a command-line tool that helps you interact with online platforms such as browsers and servers. This utility helps you install and remove packages, and manage the versions and dependencies needed to run the project.

To use packages, your project must contain a file named package.json. Inside this package, you will find metadata related to projects.

The metadata shows several aspects of the project in the following order:

- Project name
- Initial version
- Description
- Entry point
- Test commands
- Git Repository
- Keywords

- License

- Dependencies

- DevDependencies

Metadata helps identify the project and serves as the main source of information about the project.

Installation

NPM is installed with Node.js by default, so you don't need to install anything else. But you can update the installed version to the latest one. To do this, run the following command in the command line/terminal for Linux and Mac users:

```
npm install npm@latest -g
```

For Windows users, never run the above command. If you already have it, you won't be able to update npm. You will have to remove the entire Node installation.js and install again. To properly update npm in Windows, you will need to do the following. First, open PowerShell as an administrator and run the following command:

```
Set-ExecutionPolicy Unrestricted -Scope CurrentUser
-Force
```

This will ensure that the scripts run on your system. Next, you will need to install the npm-windows-upgrade utility. Once you have installed the tool, you need to run it so that it can update the npm for you. Do all this in the elevated PowerShell console.

```
npm install --global --production npm-windows--upgrade
-npm-version latest
```

To find out the current version of npm, enter the following command in the command line/terminal:

```
npm -v
```

To see if node.js is installed, open a Terminal or command-line tool and type node-v. If the package is node.js is already installed, you should see the version number:

```
node -v
```

To find out if npm is installed, enter npm-v. Again, you should see the version number:

```
npm -v
```

Node Packaged Modules

npm can install packages in local or global mode. In local mode, it installs the package in the node_modules folder in your parent working directory. This location belongs to the current user. Global packages are installed in {prefix}/lib/node_modules/which is owned by root (where {prefix} is usually /usr/ or /usr/local). This means that you will have to use sudo to install packages globally, which can lead to permission errors when resolving third-party dependencies, as well as security issues.

package.json File

The package file.json contains information about your application: name, version, dependencies, and so on. Any directory that contains this file is interpreted as a Node.a js package, even if you don't intend to publish it.

How to use the package file.json depends on whether you are going to download the package or publish it.

The package configuration file.json is used for more convenient management of the application configuration and packages in npm. So, add a new package.json file to the modulesapp project folder:

```
{
    "name": "modulesapp",
    "version": "1.0.0"
}
```

Only two sections are defined here: the project name is modulesapp and its version is 1.0.0. This is the minimum required definition of the package.json file. A given file can include many more sections.

devDependencies

In addition to the packages that are used in the application when it is running and in a working state, for example, express, that is, in the "production" state, there are also packages that are used when developing the application and testing it. Such packages are usually added to another section—devDependencies.

Downloading Packages

If you want to download the package manually, you don't need to use package.json for this. You can run the npm command in the terminal with the name of the desired package as the command argument, and the package will be automatically downloaded to the current directory. For example:

```
npm install canvas-diagram
```

You can also use package.json to download packages. Create a package file in your project directory.json, and add the following code to it (we do not specify the name of our package and version, because we are not going to publish it; we specify the name and version of the packages to download):

```
{ "devDependencies":
  {
  "canvas-diagram": "~1.4.0"
  }
}
```

Then save the file and run the npm install command in the terminal.

If you want to use many packages in your project, it is better to specify their package.json instead of downloading them every time through the terminal.

If you use package.json for downloading packages, then it turns out that you are creating a package for downloading packages. I know it's weird, but it works.

If any package has dependencies, npm will find them via package.json of the downloaded package and will download them. In our case, the canvas-diagram package also has a package.json file with the dependencies specified in it.

Publishing a Package

To publish a package, you will need to collect all the source code and the package.json file in a single directory. In the package.json, the package name, version, and dependencies must be specified. For example:

```
{
  "name": "canvas-project",
  "version": "0.1.0",
```

```
"devDependencies": {
"canvas-diagram": "~1.4.0"
}
}
```

Looking at this code, we can tell that the "canvas-project" package depends on the "canvas-diagram" package. You can publish a package using the npm publish command.

Using a Package as an Executable File

When npm downloads a package, it looks for the "bin" property in the package.json file. If it finds this property, it converts this package to an executable file and places it in the specified directory.

For example, the command below loads the grunt-cli to the current directory and converts the sources to an executable file, which is then placed in a folder with all the executable files. As a result, we will be able to call the grunt-cli command.

```
$npm install grunt-cli
```

Deleting Packages

It does not matter where the package information is located—in the dependencies or devDependencies section, the package is deleted from any of these sections.

If we need to delete more than one package, we can delete their definition from the package file.json and enter the npm install command, and removed from the package.js packages will also be removed from the node_modules folder.

For example, change the package.json file as follows:

```
{
"name": "modulesapp",
"version": "1.0.0",
"dependencies": {
}
}
```

There is no longer a definition of any packages here. And enter the command:

```
npm install
```

Moreover, we can also add some packages to the package at the same time. json, and some, on the contrary, delete. And when you run the npm install command, the package manager will install the new packages, and the deleted ones from package.json packages will be deleted.

Semantic Versioning

Semantic versioning is used to determine the package version. The version number is usually set in the following format "major.minor. patch." If a bug is found in an application or package and it is fixed, the number of "patches" is increased by one. If some new functionality is added to the package that is compatible with the previous version of the package, then this is a small change, and the number of "minor" increases. If some major changes are made to the packages that are incompatible with the previous version, the number of "major" increases. That is, looking at different versions of packages, we can assume how big the differences are in them.

GULP

Applications like Gulp belong to the so-called "task runners," as they are used to run tasks on site construction. The two most popular task managers today are Gulp and Grunt. Let's learn about their tasks and features.

Gulp is a tool for automating routine tasks that arise in web development. It can be not only frontend development, it can also be backend development.

If you implement a tool such as gulp in your work, you will significantly speed up your work. Moreover, this tool will "open the way" to new opportunities that will significantly increase your level of web development and knowledge.

Gulp is a program written in the JavaScript programming language. In order to start using it, it is desirable to know at least the basics of the JavaScript language. If you know this, then using the Gulp program will be much easier for you.

The meaning is as follows: We create certain tasks for the Gulp system. In other words, we describe these tasks in JavaScript. Then, Gulp simply performs these tasks in the desired sequence, as we have prescribed. Gulp is just a system for managing web development tasks. It is also called task manager.

It is important to understand that Gulp is just a kind of core, to which we attach additional modules, plugins that "teach" Gulp to do some specific function or work. By installing these plugins, we get new features in the Gulp system that we can use.

What typical tasks can be solved with Gulp system?
Let's look at the most basic of them.

1. **Minification of the code:** This is one of the most common tasks for which Gulp and similar systems are often used—this is the task of minifying the code. For you, this code is perceived well, but if you place this code on a working server that will host your site. Accordingly, this code will take quite a long time to load due to the fact that it has a lot of unnecessary information in the form of indents, comments, and etc.

   Gulp allows you to remove all unnecessary code, prepare it so that it can be uploaded to a working server.

2. **Combining code from different files into one:** You can combine code from CSS, JavaScript files, and others into one. This is also important because of the document loading speed. When working with the http protocol, each request to a file is an additional page load time. If you combine the code into a single file, uploading it is easier and faster than uploading multiple files. This is a typical task that has to be solved in modern web development. It is much easier to write a program if its code is divided into modules and independent parts.

3. **Working with CSS preprocessors: SASS, LESS, etc.:** The Gulp system allows you to use them in your work and you will get such a powerful tool to improve your web development skills.

4. **Support for new JavaScript language standards:** Since JavaScript is a client-side programming language, it depends on the browser it will run on. If a visitor to your site uses some old browsers, the new standards will not work for them. With Gulp, you can solve this problem.

Gulp is not the only tool that allows you to solve such similar tasks. It is important to understand that Gulp is one of the simplest and easiest solutions that allow you to do this.

The code written for Gulp is intuitive and the project that you will get is quite compact and convenient. It will have everything you need for web development.

It is safe to say that Gulp and the many utilities written for it are suitable for solving almost any task in the development of a project of any complexity—from a small site to a large project.

Any project that uses Gulp has a gulpfile file at the root.js, which contains a set of project management instructions. I would like to say right away that writing instructions for Gulp is not programming, although they are written in JavaScript. Do not be afraid of large gulpfiles.js, basically all instructions are of the same type and have common features. By the time you read this guide, you should not have any questions about Gulp, since the build system is elementary. But if you still have questions, be sure to write in the comments.

Installation

To work with Gulp, you must have installed Node.js. Installing Node.js for various platforms is quite simple—download the Node installer for your operating system and install it. I recommend installing the latest Stable version.

Attention! If you are a user of the latest version of Windows, I recommend using WSL for web development. Download the installer from the site Nodejs.org in this case, it is not necessary.

Once Node is installed, you can start installing Gulp. Open the terminal (right-click in the folder with the Shift key held down). Open the Linux shell here) and run the following command:

```
npm i gulp -g
```

For Mac and Linux users and Ubuntu bash on Windows, a global installation with the-g key must be performed with superuser rights, sudo, for example:

```
sudo npm i gulp-g
```

From this command, we can see that the npm package Manager (NPM) is launched, which uses the install command to install Gulp into the system. The-g key indicates that the package will be installed in the system globally, that is, in the system, and not in the project folder. Without the-g key, the package is installed in the folder where the current commands are executed, so be careful.

Creating a Gulp Project

Let's create a project folder for the example that we will work with, let it be, for example, the myproject folder.

Now open the terminal in the project folder. For Windows users, just hold down Shift and open the context menu. The "Open the Linux shell here" option will appear in it. The Linux shell must be pre-installed.

Next, we will initialize the project in the folder that we created:

```
npm init
```

Following the instructions, we will fill in the meta information about our project:

- Call the project "MyProject"

- Leave the current version-1.0.0

- Enter a brief description of the project—My First Gulp Project

- You can leave entry point, test command, git repository, and key-words as default

- You can also specify the author's name

- Leave the license by default and enter yes

As a result of this simple initial setup of our new Gulp project, a new package.json file will be drawn in the myproject folder.

The package file.json is a manifest file of our project, which describes in addition to the information that we have entered in the terminal, also information about the packages used in our project.

For example, if we install Gulp in the project with the—save-dev key, the package and the version used will be automatically added to our package.json. This accounting will allow you to quickly deploy a new project using an existing package.json and install the necessary modules with the dependencies that are specified in the package.json in new projects.

Let's install Gulp in our project:

```
npm i gulp --save-dev
```

What we can see from this line: npm installs the gulp package in the current myproject folder (because there is no-g key that installs the package globally into the system) and saves the package name with the version to the package.json file.

In addition, we have the node_modules folder, which now contains the installed gulp package and the necessary dependencies. This folder will automatically dump all the modules and dependencies that we will install in the project. There can be a lot of folders with dependencies, despite the fact that we have not installed so many packages, this is due to the fact that in addition to the main packages, the programs necessary for the correct operation of the main package are installed. You don't need to clean or delete anything from the node_modules folder. You may also have an additional package-lock.json file. There is nothing wrong with this, it is a service file that you can simply ignore.

Gulp SASS

Let's install the gulp-sass package in our project with the version and name saved in package.json.

Please note that any Gulp packages, for any tasks, are easily googled and have quite comprehensive connection instructions on their homepages and in the documentation.

```
npm i gulp-sass --save-dev
```

Next, we will connect gulp-sass in the file gulpfile.js. Note that variables for connecting packages can be separated by commas:

```
var gulp = require ('gulp'),
sass = require('gulp-sass'); / / Connecting the Sass
package
```

Substitutions in Node

Substitutions allow you to add more than one file to gulp.src. This is similar to regular expressions, but only for directories. When using substitutions, the computer checks the file and path names to match the pattern. If the template exists, the file is found. Most tasks typically require 4 different substitution models:

*. scss: The * character matches any template in the current directory. In our case, we are looking for all files with an ending .scss in the project root folder.

**/*.scss: This is a more advanced template that looks for files with an ending .scss in the root and all child folders.

!not-me. scss: Character! specifies that Gulp will exclude a specific file from the match result. In our case, not-me.scss will be excluded.

*.+(scss|sass): The + sign and parentheses () help to create multiple templates, the templates are separated by the | character. In our case, Gulp will find all files with an ending .scss or .sass in the root folder.

GRUNT

Based on Node.js, Grunt is a task-based command-line tool that accelerates workflow by lowering the effort required to prepare assets for production. It does this by wrapping assignments into tasks that are compiled automatically as you progress. Essentially, you can use Grunt for most tasks that you think are rough work and usually have to manually configure and run yourself. In short, Grunt is a tool for building JavaScript projects from the command line using tasks.

Why Should We Use Grunt?

One of the best features of Grunt is the consistency it brings to teams. If you've ever tried working in a team, you probably know how frustrating inconsistencies can be in your code. Grunt allows teams to work with a single set of commands, thereby ensuring that all team members write code according to the same standard. Even the smallest inconsistencies in the code, when working with a team, can bring big problems.

In addition, Grunt has a very active developers community, where new plugins are released periodically. The barrier to entrance is relatively low, since there is already a large set of tools and automated tasks.

Installation

Grunt is installed as an NPM module. If you don't have *node.js* and *npm* installed, then you need to install them. You can do this from the official site of node.js or, if you have a Mac, use homebrew. Then you need to install the *npm package manager* for node (you can draw a parallel between npm and ruby gems). Note that if you install node.js from the official website, then npm is included. You only need to install npm separately if you built node.js from source or used homebrew.

Directly installing Grunt is done with a simple *npm install-g grunt* command. The -*g* flag means global installation. Grunt will always be available from the command line, since it is installed in the *node_modules* root folder. If you want to run Grunt only in a specific folder, then while in it, run the same command without the -*g* flag.

The last step is to install the Grunt command line interface (CLI). This is what will cause the terminal to process the grunt command. Without it, running grunt will return the error "Command Not Found" (Command or file not found). It is set separately for efficiency reasons. Otherwise, if you had a dozen projects, you would have to install ten copies of GruntCLI.

Installing GruntCLI is just one line in the terminal. Just run the command:

```
npm install -g grunt-cli
```

After that, you should close and reopen the terminal window. This is generally a good approach to make sure that everything works as it should. Like how to restart your computer after installing a new program in the good old days.

Let's Make Grunt to Merge a Couple of Files

Let's imagine that our project has three separate JavaScript files:

- **jquery.js:** the library that we use

- **carousel.js:** a plugin for jQuery that we use

- **global.js:** a file written by us, where we configure and call our plugin

In production, we need to combine all these files into one to improve performance (one http request is better than three). We need to tell Grunt to do this for us.

But wait, Grunt doesn't really do anything on its own. You remember that Grunt is just a utility for performing tasks. And we will have to add the tasks themselves. So far, we haven't set up Grunt to do anything, so let's get on with it.

Official Grunt plugin for combining files is grunt-contrib-concat.

```
npm install grunt-contrib-concat --save-dev
```

A nice feature of this installation method is that the package configuration file.the json will be automatically updated and a new dependency will be written into it. Open it and make sure. A new line will appear there:

```
"grunt-contrib-concat": "~0.3.0"
```

Now we are ready to use this plugin. And to use it, we need to start setting up Grunt and telling it what to do.

You can tell Grunt what to do using a configuration file called Gruntfile .js2.

Just like the package.json file, in Gruntfile.js has its own format, which you need to adhere to. I wouldn't worry about what every word in it means. Just look at this example:

```
module.exports = function(grunt) {
// 1. The entire setup is here
grunt.initConfig({
pkg: grunt.file.readJSON('package.json'),
concat: {
// 2. The setting for combining files is here
}
});
// 3. Here we tell Grunt that we want to use this
plugin
grunt.loadNpmTasks('grunt-contrib-concat');
// 4. Specify which tasks are being performed when we
enter "grunt" in the terminal
grunt.registerTask('default', ['concat']);
};
```

Now we need to create a configuration file. The documentation can be overwhelming. Let's focus on a simple example.

Remember, we have three JavaScript files that we are trying to merge. We will list the paths to them in src as an array with the file paths (as strings in quotation marks), and then we will specify the destination file as dest. The destination file does not have to exist at this stage. It will be created in the process when the corresponding task is started, which will merge all the files into one.

And jquery.js, and carousel.js they are libraries. We probably won't change them. And, for the sake of order in the project, we will put them in a separate folder /js/libs/. File global.js—the place where we write our own code, so it will be right in the root of the /js/folder. Now you need to explain to Grunt how to find all these files and merge them into one file production.js, named to indicate that it will be used already on a real, live site.

```
concat: {
dist: {
src: [
'js/libs/*. js', / / All JS in the libs folder
'js/global.js' / / Specific file
],
dest: 'js/build/production.js',
}
}
```

The following will include the same small pieces of configuration code as this one. Their goal is to draw attention to important places, however, at first you may not understand how each piece will be integrated into a large file.

When the concat configuration is in place, open the terminal and run the command:

```
grunt
```

So, look what happens! The production.js file was created, which is an excellent combination of three files.

What Is the Difference between Gulp and Grunt?

No one likes to do boring and repetitive tasks, but the computer can do them for us. When it comes to automating the build of a front-end project, there are two main players: Grunt and Gulp. But which one to choose? What are the differences between them? Which one is better? Let's look at the main differences between Grunt and Gulp.

Grunt and Gulp are tools for building web applications, designed to automate repetitive processes such as concatenating (gluing) files, compressing images, style sheets, and JavaScript files.

Grunt and Gulp Similarities

Grunt and Gulp automate routine developer tasks, such as:

- Code minification code quality analysis

- Image optimization

- Adding vendor (browser) prefixes

- Testing

If you have tasks that repeat many times during development, you can probably automate them using Grunt or Gulp.

How does the collector perform tasks? Simply. You write instructions that tell the collector what to do:

- What files to use

- What to do with these files (minimize, concatenate, analyze for errors, etc.)

- Where to put the processed files

At first glance, Grunt and Gulp are very similar. Using any of these assemblers, you automate the web development process. More broadly, Grunt and Gulp are identical in that:

- Both automate the development process

- We write tasks using JavaScript

- Both assemblers require Node.js and npm to work

This is where the similarity ends. The method of completing tasks is different.

Differences between Grunt and Gulp

There are two main differences between Grunt and Gulp:

1. How tasks are configured. Grunt is based on the configuration. Gulp on the stream.

2. How tasks are started. Grunt runs the tasks sequentially. Gulp tries to run tasks in parallel.

Entry Limit

If we talk about getting started, then getting started with Grunt is somewhat easier, but the flip side of this coin is the difficulty of reading the settings of ready-made projects. Gulp doesn't have this drawback: the tasks in it are as easy to read as they are to write. But with enough practice, this difference is not so noticeable.

Difference in Task Configuration
Gulp's syntax is more concise than Grunt's. The great thing is that Gulp is a streaming build system. To describe tasks in Gulp, you need to write much less code.

Performing Tasks
Grunt   To execute each process in a task, Grunt must:

- Open the required file

- Start the current process

- Save·changes

- Close the currently processed file so that the next process can access it

Gulp   Gulp does not require the creation of temporary files between processes. The file, after executing the current process, is immediately transferred to the next process, without wasting time on saving the file.

Gulp uses Orchestrator, which helps to run processes as parallel as possible. This means that Gulp tries to complete all the tasks at the same time. In theory, this allows Gulp to perform tasks faster.

Plugins   In terms of the number of plugins, Gulp is noticeably inferior to Grunt, but this may well be due to the fact that Gulp is younger than its counterpart. Here are some plugins for Grunt that help you optimize your work:

- **grunt-contrib-watch:** starts tasks when the monitored files are changed.

- **grunt-contrib-jshint:** performs validation of JavaScript files.

- **grunt-mocha:** used for testing using the Mocha framework.

- **grunt-notify:** automatically shows a message when a task error occurs.

- **grunt-contrib-uglify:** minimizes files using UglifyJS.

Gulp also has all of them. There is also a gulp-grunt plugin for Gulp that allows you to run Grunt files. It does not create a stream, but is called as an argument:

```
var gulp = require ('gulp');
require ('gulp-grunt') (gulp); / / add all gruntfile
tasks to gulp

// defining tasks...
gulp.task('do-this', function () {
...
});

// run tasks
gulp task. task ('default', [
//run complete grunt tasks
'grunt - minify',
'grunt-test',
/ /run specific targets
'grunt - sass: dist',
' grunt-browserify: dev'
]);
```

Development Activity

To evaluate the software, you can see how often it is updated. If the tool is constantly being worked on, errors are corrected in it, then it will turn out to be of higher quality. Looking at the Github repositories of Grunt and Gulp, we can get an idea of the level of developer activity.

Commits occur every time the code has been updated. This can show how actively the developers are working on the project.

Github Gulp

Github Gulp

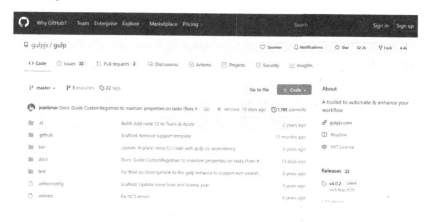

GitHub Grunt

GitHub Grunt

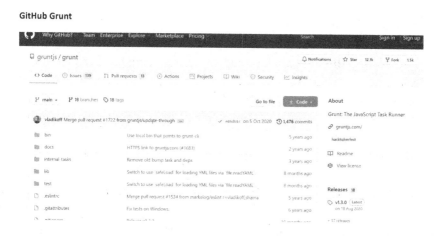

Gulp has 1195 commits and 22 releases, while Grunt has 1476 commits and 18 releases at the time of writing.

Given all of the above, which collector to choose: Grunt or Gulp? First, we don't advise you to switch to Gulp or Grunt simply because someone is trying to convince you of the extraordinary benefits of one of them. The differences are not so important if you personally are not comfortable working with the much-vaunted collector.

Secondly, when choosing between Grunt and Gulp, consider your needs. Grunt is easy to use, and you do not need to delve into the features of a complex pipe system, and the execution of simple tasks is quite clear. Grunt is a mature product with many plugins that is used by a large number of developers. At the same time, it has disadvantages such as too complex to read configuration files or slowing down when there are a large number of files due to repeated I/O operations.

Gulp, in turn, is very flexible. It is, of course, younger, but now it has all the main plugins available from Grunt. In addition, the ability to perform tasks synchronously is what you need if you are working with a large number of files. But if you haven't used NodeJS before, you may have some problems with threads at first.

As you can see, the choice between Grunt and Gulp is more a matter of personal preference. If you have never worked with assemblers, once again weigh all the pros and cons above—they will help you decide on the choice of a tool for automating your work.

Summing Up...

Grunt is written in JavaScript, uses Node.js and is supported by different platforms. The software has plugins for: reducing JavaScript and CSS, integrating pre-processors for CSS and JavaScript such as Sass/Compass, Less and Stylus, CoffeeScript or LiveScript SASS/Compass, optimizing the size of PNG and JPEG image files and automatically embedding images, and many other useful things for your work. With Grunt, you can create your own quality product. On the official website, you can find links to all possible plugins and start using them. In addition, this product will become an indispensable assistant when writing large web applications. What are its features: The program integrates optimizations for Require.js and Google Closure Compiler, allows precompilation of Handlebars, Jade, Underscore, Mustache, Eco, or Hogan templates. There are plugins for popular frameworks for testing-Jasmine, Mocha, QUnit, and Cucumber.

Gulp is another project builder that speeds up development by automating task launches. It has a large number of plugins. It also allows you to manage JavaScript files and configure the launch of tasks by other tasks.

Gulp.js uses code instead of configurations. This makes it easier to manage. For fast operation, use stream. It differs from Grunt in that instead of creating an input/output for each plugin, Gulp passes the source files through all the installed plugins to then create the output file.

Gulp is based on the principle of data streaming, which gives a lot more control over what happens and gets rid of intermediate folders and files. You pass the file to gulp, then only save the result to another file. This scheme is simple and easy to use.

In the Gulp assemblers, since it is newer, the developers have done everything not to repeat the shortcomings of Grunt in it. First, you do not need to use the watch plugin, the function of responding to changes in files is already in the kernel. It uses simple and clear JavaScript code, and in Grunt, the configuration files resemble a JSON object. Well, in Grunt, tasks work with files instead of data streams, and in Gulp, as already mentioned above, the work is based on data streaming, which is much more convenient.

CHART.JS

Chart.js

Often, people do not perceive the data presented in the form of text or tables. First, because it is boring, but much more so because it is more difficult to understand the value of the numbers presented in this form. Even if the table is small, there is still a chance that a person will run through it and miss some information. As a rule, the user will look carefully only at a couple of countries that interest him more than others. If the same data were presented in the form of a diagram, a person could easily see the whole picture, namely, the ratio of the population of different countries.

When we are dealing with charts, it is much easier for us to identify a trend or fact. For example, just look at the graph, and it will immediately become clear that the population of the United States is twice as large as in Bangladesh, and the number of people living in China is ten times more than the population of Russia.

Chart.js is a popular tool that is designed for creating graphs and charts. This series of lessons will cover all aspects of working with this library. You can create adaptive charts of any complexity based on HTML5 Canvas.

This library allows you to easily create graphs and charts of any type, as well as build data on a time range and logarithmic scale. It also has built-in tools for working with animation, which will allow you to effectively modify the graphics depending on new data, as well as experiment with color.

Let's start with the installation, and then deal with the configuration and other settings.

Installation

You can download the latest version of Chart.js with GitHub or connect the library to your project using the CDN link. You can also install via npm or bower by running one of the following commands:

```
npm install chart.js --save
bower install chart.js -save
```

The source code is available in two trim levels. Full version of the Chart. js and stripped down Chart.min.js, which includes the Chart library.js and color palette parser. If you select the second option, you will have to go to Chart to create charts with a time scale.js separately connect the Moment.js.

In the version that comes as Chart. bundle.js or Chart.bundle.min.js, Moment.js is already connected. This will save you from having to attach multiple separate files. Just make sure that the Moment.js will not be loaded twice. This can lead to a library version conflict.

Now that we have decided which version of the library we will work with, we can connect the code and start creating cool diagrams.

```
< script src="path/to/Chart.min.js"></script>
```

```
<script>
var barChart = new Chart({...})
</script>
```

CHOREOGRAPHER.JS

Choreographer.js

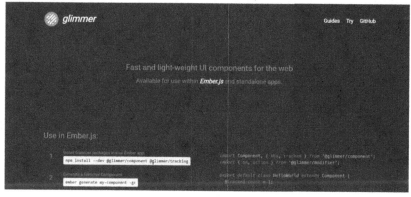

Choreographer.js is a simple JavaScript library for CSS animation. It's easy to use, and it really helps you create complex CSS animations for your site.

Installation

You can install Choreographer.js via typing the following command:

`npm install - save choreographer-js`

GLIMMER.JS

Glimmer.js

Glimmer.js is a great library that helps with user interface components and DOM rendering. It is built on the Ember CLI and uses Git, Node. js, npm, and Yarn. If you are looking for a tool for creating components and want to optimize the process of working with them, pay attention to Glimmer.

Installation

You can install Glimmer in Ember apps like this:

```
npm install --dev @glimmer/component @glimmer/tracking
```

You can install Glimmer also the following way:

```
npm install -g ember-cli
```

GRANIM.JS

Granim.js

Decorate the background of your site with a colorful gradient using Granim.js. This small JavaScript library is perfect for adding smooth and interactive gradients. You can use them independently of other elements, or you can use them to cover an image or place them under a graphic mask.

ANIME.JS

Anime.js

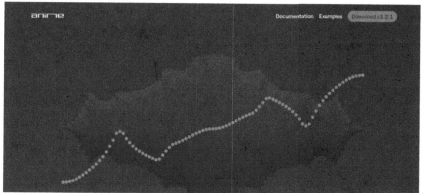

Animation.js and micro-interactions are now trending. Anime.js will add some traffic to the site. Anime.js is a lightweight JavaScript animation library with a simple but powerful API. It works with CSS properties, Scalable Vector Graphics (SVG), DOM attributes, and JavaScript objects.

It has a list of features, some of which are

- Step-by-step system built into the anime makes it easy to work through complex and overlapping animations. It can be used for both timings and properties.

- Animating multiple CSS conversion properties with different time-stamps simultaneously in a single HTML element.

- Play, pause, control, reverse, and trigger events synchronously using the full built-in callback and control functions.

- It works with any website. Animate all CSS, SVG, DOM attributes, as well as JavaScript objects using a single unified API.

AOS—ANIMATION ON SCROLL.JS

AOS - Animation on Scroll.js

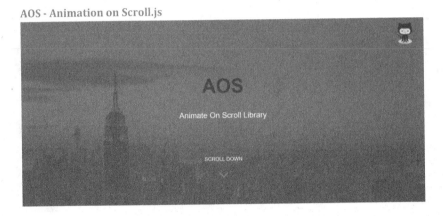

Are you working on a single-page website with the parallax effect? Animate on Scroll adds a nice animation when scrolling the page. This library will help you create an attractive design: it has everything from fade effects to static bindings.

BIDEO.JS

Bideo.js

Full-screen videos serve as a great background for the site. Bideo.js—JavaScript library for adding a video phone that looks good on a screen of any size and scales smoothly.

CLEAVE.JS

Cleave.js

Have you ever used a form field that would format content while typing? For example, to turn 1020304050 into a phone number with an international code: (102) 030-4050. Cleave.js is a JavaScript library that allows you to add similar functions to your site.

THREE.JS

Three.js

Three.js is a really interesting JavaScript library for those interested in three-dimensional design. Check out the Paper Planes website—where you can throw paper planes with your phone.

VOCA.JS

Voca makes it easier to work with strings by offering useful functions like case-changing, clipping, and truncating. The library is divided into several modules, which allows you to work with its individual functions.

TWEEN.JS

Tween is a part of the CreateJS package and, as such, is incredibly efficient for creating animations in HTML and JavaScript.

SLICK.JS

Slick.js

Slick will help you realize the carousel effect. It has a full array of options, works with swipe gestures for mobile devices, and supports other cool features. You can even sync the two carousels if you want to create an overlay effect.

CONCLUSION

That brings us to the end of this book about Node frameworks. We started off by discussing the very concept of JavaScript frameworks, how they work, what they are useful for, and so on.

Following that, we took a while to understand the basics of Node.js such as its uses, installation and features. We then turned our attention toward Node and its server-side usage, as well as the concepts of Node modules.

Once done with that, we then explored numerous Node.js frameworks, such as Polymer, Aurelia, Svelte, Webix, Conditioner.js, and so on.

Lastly, we turned toward JS tools such as task managers (npm) and task runners like Gulp or Grunt. Furthermore, we also discussed in brief several smaller libraries, pertaining to certain niche functions and concepts.

Now that you have finished reading this book, we hope it will prove useful to you in your journey of JavaScript. Happy coding!

Index

Printed in the United States
by Baker & Taylor Publisher Services